Corporate Interiors

No. 8

Corporate Interiors

No. 8

Roger Yee

Visual Reference Publications Inc., New York

Opposite: An Investment Management Company, Chicago, Illinois. **Design firm:** VOA Associates Incorporated. **Photography:** Nick Merrick/Hedrich Blessing.

Corporate Interiors No. 8

Visual Reference Publications, Inc.
302 Fifth Avenue • New York, NY 10001
Tel: 212.279.7000 • Fax: 212.279.7014 • Fax: 212.279.7014

www.visualreference.com

GROUP PUBLISHER	Larry Fuersich larry@visualreference.com
PUBLISHER	Bill Ash bill@visualreference.com
EDITORIAL DIRECTOR	Roger Yee yeerh@aol.com
CREATIVE ART DIRECTOR	Veronika Cherepanina veronika@visualreference.com
ASSISTANT ART DIRECTOR	Shannon Linde shannon@visualreference.com
PRODUCTION MANAGER	John Hogan johnhvrp@yahoo.com
CIRCULATION MANAGER	Amy Yip amy@visualreference.com
MARKETING COORDINATOR	Nika Chopra nika@visualreference.com
CONTROLLER	Angie Goulimis angie@visualreference.com
ADMINISTRATOR	Irene Band irene@visualreference.com

Library of Congress Cataloging in Publication Data: Corporate Interiors No. 8

ISBN: 978-1-58471-110-0   ISBN: 1-58471-110-8

Distributors to the trade in the United States and Canada
Watson-Guptill
770 Broadway
New York, NY 10003

Distributors outside the United States and Canada
HarperCollins International
10 East 53rd Street
New York, NY 10022-5299

Exclusive distributer in China
Beijing Designerbooks Co., Ltd.
Building No.2, No.3, Babukou, Gulouxidajie,
Xicheng District, Beijing 100009, P.R.China
Tel: 0086(010)6406-7653 Fax: 0086(010)6406-0931
E-mail: info@designerbooks.net www.designerbooks.net

Printed and bound in China

Book Design: Veronika Levin

Naòs System. Studio Cerri & Associati
Pierluigi Cerri
Alessandro Colombo

Photo Mario Carrieri

UNIFOR
149 Fifth Avenue
New York, NY 10010
tel. 212 673 3434
fax 212 673 7317
e-mail: unifor@uniforusa.com

UNIFOR

thinkglobal™

value is always in style.™

Contents

Teknion

What will the next generation say of us? That we stepped forward to begin to shape a sustainable future? Or, that we lacked the daring to take up the task of changing how we work, play, build and consume. At Teknion, we believe that every leap forward is the sum of many steps.

The products we introduce in 2007 represent the emerging values of sustainable thinking: **District,** a furniture-based systems alternative that makes more out of small spaces and preserves an open, light-filled setting; **Marketplace,** a reinvention of the worktable that minimizes barriers to interaction and makes efficient use of space and materials; and **Optos,** a glass wall system designed to allow a path for natural light transmission while providing territorial and acoustical privacy. Small moves, such as these, can lead us towards our larger goal.

Today, we will do less harm. Tomorrow — or the day after — all of the things we make will be designed to create a world that is safe, healthy and humane. Whatever we can do, let us begin it now.

Teknion small moves, big shift

Teknion

A modular desking system

www.teknion.com

Small moves, big shift

Teknion
Teknion District

Project: Yale University Art Gallery Renovation, New Haven, CT
Original Building Architect: Louis Kahn
Original Building Lighting Design: Richard Kelly
Renovation Architect: Polshek Partnership Architects
Renovation Lighting Design: Fisher Marantz Stone
Exhibition Lighting Design: Hefferan Partnership Lighting Design
Lighting Manufacturer: Lighting Services Inc

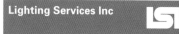

Teknion

Teknion Marketplace

03

Design: Carl Gustav Magnusson

www.teknion

Small moves, big shift

versteel environments

A **FULL SPECTRUM** OF PRODUCTS TO MEET YOUR NEEDS.

A variety of personal workstations, seating, and support products allow you to SPECIFY ENTIRE ENVIRONMENTS from a single source. Visit us at **versteel.com** to find out more about our extensive product offering.

VERSTEEL.
Building more than a great table.

ODIS

AN INDIVIDUAL STACKING TABLE FOR **"ON DEMAND"** WORK SURFACES.

ODIS is lightweight and easily stacked on the floor or transport. A seamless surface of wood or laminate rolls over the edge to form the modesty panel and optional PERSONAL STORAGE can be added to each table. 32 standard powder coat colors, 1000's of standard laminates and 11 wood finishes will **MAKE A STATEMENT** in any environment.

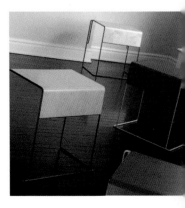

CALL **800 876 2120** OR VISIT **versteel.com**

*I*ntroduction

High Energy, Low Fat

A new type of workplace is emerging in our time.

Nice work—if you can get it.

Consumer confidence surveys reveal Americans are getting worried about the availability of jobs even as corporate America complains about the lack of people able and willing to do its work for the going rate of pay. Who's right? It's true that companies like Caterpillar are rushing to train young service technicians to replace retiring ones, and Halliburton wants petroleum engineers badly enough to let them write their own ticket. On the other hand, business leaders are still aggressively cutting expenditures for personnel and the facilities to house them. While IBM has gone on a hiring spree in India, where 53,000 employees currently focus on research, software and services, it has eliminated 15,000 positions in Europe and 3,500 more in the United States. The newest offices being developed by leading architects and interior designers for major businesses and institutions reflect this ambivalence.

Surprisingly, "lean and mean" may not be the first words that come to mind when you see the latest generation of offices. Since the walls and doors increasingly consist of modular and reusable components that are made in the factory and assembled in the field, they project a cool, precise and high-tech image. Private offices continue to line the building's perimeter, but are heavily or fully enclosed in glass to let daylight penetrate the building's interior. Open workstations, separated from each other by low-height partitions that no longer pretend to furnish visual and acoustical privacy, offer unimpeded views that may include the outdoors. Modest as these individual offices often are, they are complemented by more spacious meeting areas that encourage group interaction with versatile furnishings, advanced IT tools, and food and beverages. Overall, the new offices embody utility, comfort and responsiveness. They look good too, because business now appreciates the power of design to transform everything from an Apple iPhone to a Ferrari 599 GTB Fiorano.

However, make no mistake about their purpose. Ornamented by small, deliberate applications of fine materials and furnishings, standardized in space and materials for all employees, and outfitted with temporarily assigned "touchdown" stations as well as permanently assigned private offices or cubicles, the 21st century office is all business. Corporate America won't encounter much physical resistance when it's time to change layouts or vacate the premises. The old symbols of opulence, formality and permanence are nowhere in sight.

Executives must know that employees are generally quite perceptive about the new workplace. No one comes here to retire with a gold watch. But if the architecture and interior design are well suited to the organizations they serve, they will help orient, enable and motivate people so they can excel at their work, feel good about their employers, and acquire new knowledge and skills. That's what readers will see from the nation's leading architects and interior designers in the pages of *Corporate Interiors No. 8*: Space that works.

Roger Yee

Editor

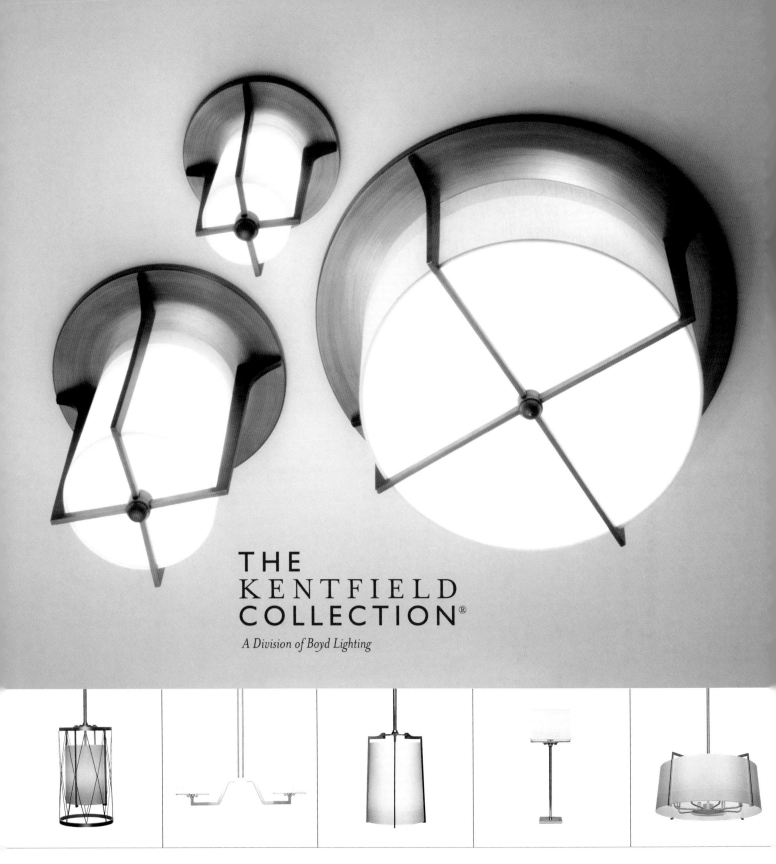

THE
KENTFIELD
COLLECTION®

A Division of Boyd Lighting

New ceiling fixtures now available in the Soleil Collection by Jiun Ho

THE KENTFIELD COLLECTION

866.251.7777 | kentfieldcollection.com

Aref & Associates

100 N. Sepulveda Blvd.
Suite 100
El Segundo, CA 90245
310.414.1000
310.414.1099 (Fax)
www.aref.com

Aref & Associates

Aref & Associates

Tradewinds Global Investors
Los Angeles, California

Top: Reception.
Left: Reception seating area.
Below: Trading desks.
Bottom: Private Office.
Opposite: Main reception entry.
Photography: Paul Bielenberg.

Investors are becoming increasingly adventurous in crossing political boundaries in the 21st century. To dramatize the financial industry's unprecedented freedom to take equity positions almost anywhere in the world, Tradewinds Global Investors recently decided to focus on an international theme for its new, one-floor, 26,000-square-foot office in the Century City district of Los Angeles, California, designed for over 90 employees by Aref & Associates. The layout is typical of those favored by financial firms, comprising private offices for analysts and portfolio managers with open trading desks for traders, and open workstations for administrative personnel, along with a reception area, conference center, and a commons-style staff lounge. However, the contemporary design is both timeless and accented with such exotic materials and furnishings as limestone flooring from France, Onyx stone in reception, a one-of-a-kind console table from Shanghai, and original works of art in various media from artists in Europe, Asia, Africa and the Americas. With ample interior glass, flexible, ergonomic furnishings, and warm direct/indirect lighting, the space also enables people to work under optimum conditions while encouraging them to collaborate at all levels. For Tradewinds, a respected manager of assets for institutions and private clients worldwide, it's the right place at the right time.

Aref & Associates

The Staubach Company
Los Angeles, California

When legendary Dallas Cowboys quarterback Roger Staubach founded The Staubach Company in 1977, he built the Dallas-based commercial real estate advisory firm with the same confidence he displayed on the gridiron, exclusively representing users of office, industrial and retail space at a time few brokers knew about "user representation." Corporate customers embraced the strategy. Today, 1,400 employees in over 60 North American offices represent clients across the continent, while the DTZ Staubach Tie Leung partnership has 11,800 professionals overseas serving clients worldwide. Thoughtful action has also rewarded Staubach's Los Angeles office, where a new, one-floor, 19,000-square-foot space, designed by Aref & Associates, welcomed roughly 73 employees from an environment of private offices to one with just open plan workstations. Of course, the transformation accommodates privacy and heavy telephone usage. Senior brokers occupy workstations along the window wall separated by glass walls while others work in interior workstations, and staff and visitors share use of such generous public spaces as a reception area, conference rooms, team rooms and staff lounge. The bold, contemporary facility, appointed in bird's eye maple, marble and glass with versatile, team-oriented furnishings and direct/indirect lighting, has scored well with brokers and Mr. Staubach himself.

Right: Reception and main conference room.
Below: Senior Broker's Workstation.
Bottom left: Broker's Work-space.
Bottom right: Reception.
Opposite bottom: Club House.
Photography: Paul Bielenberg.

Aref & Associates

Sempra Energy - Southern California Gas Company
Monterey Park, California

Can a 120-degree arc actually improve office operations? To enhance the efficiency, interactivity and flexibility of its 125-person office in Monterey Park, California, Sempra Energy recently unveiled a new, one-floor, 29,000-square-foot workspace based on a 120-degree, all-open plan configuration, designed by Aref & Associates. The hexagonal geometry of the workstations, a departure from the 90-degree orthogonal grid generally used in open plan offices, better addresses employee functions for the utility company. Combined with team rooms framed in demountable walls for easy redeployment, video conference rooms, telephone rooms and cyber café, the distinctive open plan areas sustain an environment that is both functional and interactive. The substantial distance between the hub of the office and the exterior windows on the large floor plate is not obvious to the work force, interestingly enough, because the design compensates for this condition by introducing skylights and direct and indirect lighting in various areas to add a warm ambiance. Going a step further, the award-winning design makes such inspired use of sustainable materials and furnishings

that it has been granted LEED Gold certification. Sempra employees give the company high marks for the new facility, where innovative form and function are making a discernable difference.

Top: Conference center.
Above left: Open plan area with skylight.
Above right: Collaborative space and team rooms.
Opposite: Cyber café.
Photography: Paul Bielenberg.

22

Aref & Associates

Steptoe & Johnson LLP
Los Angeles, California

When Los Angelenos talk about "the industry," they refer to the entertainment industry, which has sprawled well beyond its historic center in Hollywood over the course of eight decades. Serving "the industry" calls for highly specialized skill and expertise, and the strong entertainment practice maintained by the Los Angeles law office of Steptoe & Johnson is reflected in its new, 1 ½-floor, 33,000-square-foot office, designed by Aref & Associates. To give Steptoe's approximately 90 attorneys and administrative staff an effective workplace, the design establishes a warm, inviting yet cutting edge environment that entertainment industry people can appreciate. The reception area, private offices for attorneys, secretarial workstations, conference rooms, war rooms and computer room are appointed in finishes that contrast wood veneers and warm carpet against cool stone flooring, neutral clear glass and vibrant artwork, modern, ergonomic furnishings, and direct and indirect lighting fixtures such as pendants and wall sconces. If the sleek image of the space inspires thoughts of sophistication, comfort and drama at the same time—all intensified by panoramic views of Los Angeles from the windows—clients of the respected, 94-year-old firm should feel confident that they've come to the right attorneys for service.

Top right: Open plan area.
Middle right: Video conference screen in main conference room
Above: Main conference room.
Left: Main reception area.
Photography: Paul Bielenberg.

BBG-BBGM

515 Madison Avenue
4th Floor
New York, NY 10022
212.888.7663
212.935.3868 (Fax)
www.bbg-bbgm.com

1825 K Street NW
Suite 300
Washington DC 20006
202.452.1644
202.452.1647 (Fax)

BBG-BBGM

BBG-BBGM

Blue Heron Capital
Washington, D.C.

Natural light adds much vitality to the new, one-floor, 7,000-square-foot Washington,D.C. office for the 12 employees of Blue Heron Capital, a venture capital firm. The visitor never notices that 70 percent of the window-facing space parallels a narrow alley offering very little sunlight. Fortunately, the design by BBG-BBGM fully exploits the 10 percent of the office that draws in plenty of daylight. To convey this daylight deep into the office, which comprises a reception area, private offices, formal conference room, team rooms, and client and employee lounge, full glass is used to create a virtually transparent core to house the three meeting facilities. Not only does the transparency provide total visual contact from one side to the other, but it also transmits direct and indirect daylight denied to the alley-facing windows. This adroit play on light and transparency is reinforced by the selection of a vivid color palette, reclaimed wood floor, and light, stylish contemporary furnishings, that help space turn a potential design liability into an asset for this strategically situated office—just two blocks north of the White House.

Top left: Formal conference room.
Above: Reception.
Right: Client and employee lounge.
Photography: Jeffrey Totaro.

BBG-BBGM

Institute of Transportation Engineers
Washington, D.C.

After occupying the same building for 20 years, the Institute of Transportation Engineers (ITE), an international educational and scientific association of transportation professionals, recently took a journey of its own by developing a new, one-floor, 14,000-square-foot office in Washington, D.C., designed by BBG-BBGM. The relocation of 56 staff members to a modern, functional and attractive facility, consisting of a reception area, private offices, multi-function conference room, and training and fulfillment center, acknowledges the Institute's broad membership and supports its dynamic new agenda. To support its many activities, the design embraces a clean, northern European aesthetic of subdued colors, maple wood and aluminum finishes, and contemporary furnishings, creating quality workplaces for both the executive offices and general working area, which are physically separate. It also neatly resolves the challenge of honoring past and future presidents by displaying their photographs in a sleek, double-curved wall with 90 openings, including 70 for past presidents and 20 for the next 20 years. This low-key solution blends into the overall scheme without diminishing the importance of the images, and is one of numerous details that sustains a dynamic environment.

Below: Multi-function conference room.

Opposite: Gallery of Presidents.

Photography: Jeffrey Totaro.

28

BBG-BBGM

Four Seasons Venture Capital
Washington, D.C.

Right: Exterior view.

Below: Private office in see-through view.

Opposite: Project conference room in lobby.

Photography: Jeffrey Totaro.

The thought of working in a goldfish bowl may not appeal to everyone. Yet, the concept has served Four Seasons Venture Capital well in its new Washington, D.C. office, located in the fashionable Georgetown neighborhood. Because Four Seasons chose to occupy the ground floor of an office building across from a picturesque and well-traveled path along Georgetown's historic canal, its one-floor, 5,000-square-foot space, designed by BBG-BBGM, would be in full view of the public. However, the venture capital firm wanted to bring as much light inside the workplace as possible and did not consider the exposure to be a constraint. Therefore, the design team created a totally transparent space where each private office not only borrows light from the outside, it shares the light with neighboring offices—facilitating visual communication between office occupants—and interior areas via clear glass walls. (Besides private offices, the space houses a lobby and project conference room, executive conference room, and lounge.) Treating the offices as the company's "façade," the design makes every visual element count in the overall image, from bold colors and glass-and-aluminum-framed walls to open, contemporary furnishings. For 12 employees, Georgetown opens an inviting window to the world with views both ways.

BBG-BBGM

Edelman Financial Services
Fairfax, Virginia

Left: Main reception area.

Below left: Corridor.

Below right: Executive suite seen through "fins" in main reception area.

Photography: Jeffrey Totaro.

Clients arriving at the new, one-floor, 19,000-square-foot office of Edelman Financial Services, in Fairfax, Virginia, are not mistaken in feeling at home even though the facility is clearly a place for conducting business. That's because the handsomely appointed space, which encompasses an executive suite, private offices, open workstations, IT center, staff lounge, and coffee bars, has been designed by BBG-BBGM for 80 employees of a firm founded by Ric Edelman. Edelman, a successful financial planner with a popular radio program, a nationally syndicated newspaper column, and best-selling author, wanted to project an intimate yet professional image.

Consequently, highly visible areas like the reception area and lobby take on a residential character with urbane and sophisticated sofas and armchairs, subdued lighting, and works of art on the walls. How does the environment actually function? Apparently the soothing and professional air of the office is fostering communication and client interaction, just as Edelman intended. In fact, Edelman Financial Services is using the design as a prototype for a national expansion.

DMJM Rottet

Los Angeles
515 South Flower Street, 8th Floor
Los Angeles, CA 90071
213.593.8300

Houston
808 Travis Street, Suite 100
Houston, TX 77002
713.221.1830

San Francisco
405 Howard Street, 4th Floor
San Francisco, CA 94105
415.986.1373

Washington D.C.
3101 Wilson Boulevard
Arlington, VA 22201
703.682.4900

New York
605 Third Avenue
New York, NY 10158
212.973.2900

Shanghai
30F Shanghai Times Square
No. 93 Huaihai Zhong Road
Shanghai, China 200021
86.21.6391.0303

www.dmjmrottet.com

DMJM Rottet

Lime Rock Management
Houston, Texas

DMJM Rottet's design of Lime Rock Management's new 16,000-square-foot Houston office succeeds by achieving two key goals for the energy investment firm. It simultaneously distinguishes and physically separates the firm's two operating teams while maintaining common areas for collaboration and entertainment that effectively brand the space. Because program requirements demanded space planning efficiencies to accommodate rapid growth plans and the highly collaborative nature of the business, the design features an imaginative environment with two interior "floating glass boxes" to house individual offices. Folding planes of glass, wood, color, and art collectively enclose the "boxes," combining privacy and daylight and blurring the distinction between wall, floor, ceiling, and furniture. All materials, furnishings, and art reflect Lime Rock's activities, including the vintage images of oil derricks collected by DMJM Rottet that reflect both the energy industry and the building's cross bracing. The design team also worked with a local artist to create a ceiling sculpture to emulate rock formations. Committed to providing an inspiring office environment for its employees and guests, Lime Rock is gratified by ongoing praise for the results. As employees explain, "This is not an office, but an environment in which we work and have fun."

Top: Entry from Building Corridor.

Middle: Corridor and View Towards "Oil Upshot".

Bottom: Informal seating and reception area.

Opposite: Reception Desk from Portal.

Photography: Benny Chan/ Fotoworks.

DMJM Rottet

Executive Offices for a Fortune 100 Company
Norwalk, Connecticut

When the executives of a Fortune 100 company chose DMJM Rottet to design their 88,000-square-foot office on the two penthouse floors of the company's new 360,000-square-foot headquarters building in Norwalk, Connecticut, they requested an environment combining architectural beauty with technical sophistication. In response, the design team created an elliptical wood staircase suspended from bronze clad metal rods as the primary architectural focus. DMJM Rottet worked with a local vendor to perfect Italian plaster finishes, and meticulously detailed interiors of glass, stone, carpet, and naturally reclaimed wood to create visual highlights in such spaces as the reception area, the dining room, and the coffee lounge overlooking the reception area. The client's goals of sophistication, functionality, and technological advancement are exemplified in the conference center. Here, the main boardroom features banquette seating integrated into the two long walls, custom-made cabinetry, a dramatic wood ceiling, and state-of-the-art conferencing technology that is now the prototype for company offices worldwide. DMJM Rottet furthered the client's sustainability objectives by enabling natural light to penetrate the space through the use of transparent office walls, a two-story reception area, skylights, and perimeter light-wells. The office is currently registered with the U.S. Green Building Council in anticipation of LEED certification.

Top: Stair Landing.
Middle: Conference Room.
Bottom: Front Desk.
Opposite: View Inside Stairwell.
Photography: Benny Chan/ Fotoworks.

36

DMJM Rottet

Paul, Hastings, Janofsky & Walker LLP
Washington, D.C.

The Washington, D.C. office of Paul, Hastings, Janofsky & Walker, an international law firm of some 1,100 attorneys in 18 offices, feels at home in its new, 75,000-square-foot law office, designed by DMJM Rottet. Although the D.C. office incorporates many of the standards developed by DMJM Rottet for the firm's offices in Los Angeles and New York, its location in the historic Bowen Building posed unique opportunities and challenges. To locate the new conference center and reception area in the building's soaring lobby, for example, the design team used the extreme height to bring daylight deep inside. A newly installed "shuttle elevator" connecting the lobby to the typical floors above gives the impression that the entire building is occupied by Paul Hastings- -an image that supports its stature in the legal community. The architecture of the lobby epitomizes the merging of the "old" and the "new." Upstairs, light wood veneers and low contrasting finishes help overcome the building's tight floors, and a modification of the existing exit stair creates an atrium-like skylight that is opened throughout Paul Hastings' top floors. The result, from top to bottom, is a bright, lofty and efficient environment for 103 attorneys and support staff.

Top: Mezzanine.

Bottom: Reception.

Opposite: Conference Room.

Photography: Hedrich Blessing/ Nick Merrick.

DMJM Rottet

Cushman & Wakefield
Los Angeles, California

When Cushman & Wakefield decided to relocate its Westside Los Angeles office, it posed several challenges to DMJM Rottet. The design team was asked to create a 10,000-square-foot work environment that would appeal to the company's broad client base, including many entertainment industry clients, and to reflect the company's premier image in the industry. Moreover, the new office had to be completed on a tight schedule and moderate budget. The design focuses on the reception area, where the contemporary look that reflects the company's progressive outlook is also deliberately warm and inviting. Its warm wood accents, limestone floors, and white modern furniture create a high contrast space with residential overtones. Budget-conscious design extras such as cutouts in the drywall give hints to the conference room beyond and create a sense of movement and energy. The glazing at the entry, clerestory, and slots provides glimpses of the space beyond, but maintain privacy by shielding critical items. Even with the need to create a marquee space within a limited area, modest budget, and aggressive move-in schedule, DMJM Rottet created a workplace that not only serves this premier brokerage firm and its customers, it showcases what real estate can become.

Top left: Detail of Reception.
Top right: Administrative Corridor.
Bottom: Reception.
Photography: Hedrich Blessing/ Nick Merrick.

EwingCole

Federal Reserve Bank Building
100 North 6th Street
Philadelphia, PA 19106
215.923.2020
215.351.5346 (Fax)
www.ewingcole.com

EwingCole

Olympus America Inc.
Headquarters
Center Valley, Pennsylvania

Who could track a moving target better than a respected maker of digital cameras, research microscopes, and other advanced medical imaging systems? For Olympus America, the North American arm of Japan's Olympus, the recent relocation of its headquarters from New York's Long Island to Pennsylvania's Lehigh Valley inspired a thorough assessment of internal departmental structure and staffing needs as part of its agile business plan. As a result, the architecture and interior design of Olympus America's new, three-floor,

Above: Exterior.

Right: Walkway.

Opposite: Lobby.

Photography: Jeff Totaro, Noah Webb.

337,400-square-foot headquarters on 54 acres in Center Valley, designed by EwingCole for 650 employees (with room for 950), will sustain years of change. The project was complicated by a tight schedule, which required that programming and design proceed simultaneously. However, the schedule's rigor not only required resolving potential delays resulting from the continual reevaluation of business and operating models, it helped shape the efficient, "one-size-fits-all" developer model adopted to integrate operating groups and maximize flexibility. In fact, placing work stations in open, column-free space—just seven offices are fully-enclosed—enabled Olympus America to open on time by concentrating specialized spaces in public areas, including such facilities as the lobbies, showrooms, 400-seat conference center, and dining hall, in core space, where small conference rooms, file areas, pantries

EwingCole

and copy centers can be found, or separate areas such as the research laboratories and manufacturing/warehouse. Yet the floor plan is just one of the building's fresh concepts. For example, the raised floor functions as a platform for under-floor air, power and data distribution—a flexible, energy-efficient and noiseless alternative to conventional infrastructure. The 7,000-square-foot data center exists as a secure building within a building, using separate M/E and teledata systems. The metal-and-glass curtainwall is equipped with solar screening mullion extensions and lighting controls to regulate perimeter cove lighting during the transition from daylight to darkness, while expansive glass windows and open, column-free interiors bring daylight and views of the surrounding woods and seven-acre lake to all employees. Finally, the building supports an exceptional working environment. Responding to the company's needs at multiple levels, it reinforces the Olympus brand through sleek modern design that evokes Japanese aesthetics, offers such intuitive wayfinding cues as the perimeter main circulation path, and operates a child care center, laundry/dry cleaning and other useful amenities. Observing how well the new headquarters serves Olympus America,

Mark Gumz, president and COO, declares, "Employee reaction has been overwhelmingly positive and we are poised for tremendous growth."

Right: Administrative area.
Below left: Cafeteria.
Bottom right: View from cafeteria.

EwingCole

SCA Americas Headquarters
Philadelphia, Pennsylvania

Visitors will probably not detect overt signs that SCA Americas is an international arm of a Stockholm-based leader in hygiene products, packaging and publication papers at its new, three-floor, 81,200-square-foot North American headquarters, designed by EwingCole, in Philadelphia. However, the Swedish roots of the $13-billion business, operating in over 50 countries with 51,000 employees, express themselves in understated but beneficial ways. Inspired by what began in 1929 as a forest products company "to provide essential products that improve the quality of everyday life,™" the design team has endeavored to better the lives of the 120 headquarters employees through space planning, interior architecture and engineering. The overall design, for example, is characterized by references to such basic elements of nature as earth, light and water. In addition, 93 percent of occupied spaces have access to daylight, informal breakout areas and casual spaces give employees opportunities for impromptu interaction, and materials and lighting have been carefully selected to provide a healthy work environment. More profound evidence of the Scandinavian sensibility can be seen in the workplace model, which has shifted from a traditional, formal and hierarchical order characterized by private offices to a more open, inclusive and egalitarian one. The new headquarters is characterized by a small number of private offices defined by glass walled enclosures, open-plan workstations that employ low-height partitions,

Above: Reception entry space.

Left: View of offices from reception.

Opposite: Spiral staircase.

Photography: Christopher Barrett.

EwingCole

three-story, interior staircase, spacious corridors, and informal gathering places— along with a boardroom, conference rooms, training rooms, café, lunchroom, and restrooms—all complemented by furnishings that minimize hierarchy. Equally important, SCA Americas offers an attractive and inviting workplace for employees. Taking cues from the curvilinear geometry of the Cira Centre building that houses it, elements of Scandinavian modernism that are expressed in artwork, color and wood and other natural materials, and such green design strategies as increasing access to daylight, reusing construction materials, and reducing water usage, the new headquarters has emerged as a unique setting possessing as much style as utility. In fact, such distinctive features as the interior staircase, a bold, sculptural form with an elliptical plan that mirrors the Cira Centre's architecture, have won raves from employees and visitors alike. John O'Rourke, vice president, human resources for SCA Americas, reports, "Employees are thrilled with their new space. Everybody comments on how fast the time goes. Visitors walk through the space and tell us that this is the kind of company they would like to work for."

Top left: Overhead view of staircase.
Top right: Conference room.
Left: Coffee bar.

Francis Cauffman

Francis Cauffman

McNeil Nutritionals
Fort Washington, Pennsylvania

Should a business with an innovative and action-oriented corporate culture go beyond the conventional workplace of private offices and open workstations to house its workforce? Consider the exceptional new environment designed by Francis Cauffman for McNeil Nutritionals in Fort Washington, Pennsylvania. The one-floor, 30,000-square-foot space, developed for 120 employees of the Johnson & Johnson company that produces such products as Splenda® sweetener, Viactiv® calcium soft chews, and Lactaid® milk and dietary supplements, demonstrates how effectively architecture can meet the needs of a progressive organization. Focus groups representing a cross section of personnel helped produce an "open and dynamic" spatial concept omitting enclosed offices to encourage interaction, collaboration and cross-functional teamwork. Among the design's highlights are a multifunctional entry area, serving as McNeil Nutritionals' public face with a "town hall" containing informal meeting areas, bistro and touchdown spots, 120-degree open workstations, chosen

to avoid the silo-like confinement of orthogonal arrangements and to facilitate change, open and enclosed team rooms, boardroom, innovation room, and product development and demonstration kitchen. Not only does the layout express functional needs over company hierarchy, organizational changes are accommodated without reconstruction, and

employees move themselves, projecting an energy both employees and visitors can sense.

Francis Cauffman

Greenberg Traurig, LLP
Wilmington, Delaware

Above: Open office area.

Right: Breakout room.

Below right: View of breakout room from conference room.

Opposite: Conference room.

Photography: Don Pearse.

For Greenberg Traurig, an international, full-service law firm with 1,600 attorneys and governmental affairs professionals in the United States, Europe and Asia, the space housing its new, one-floor, 17,000-square-foot office in Wilmington, Delaware could easily have yielded a confined facility with limited daylight for some 30 employees. That would hardly have suited a firm whose progressive thinking helps lawyers get outstanding results for clients. Fortunately, the light, airy and colorful environment designed by Francis Cauffman deftly compensates for an irregular floor plan handicapped by a multi-story light well, large columns, sizable core and low finished ceiling height. The key to the solution has been to introduce transparency through interior glass walls and to supplement daylight by illuminating walls and coves in a naturalistic way. Because of these and other design details in the classic modern space, which is appointed in wood, glass, marble and contemporary furnishings, the office is a model of openness and light. Says Michele Tigue Daly, business director of Greenberg Traurig, "We were looking for a design that was different than the traditional law firm, a design that was more in tune with Greenberg Traurig's culture. The end result was even better than what we had envisioned."

Francis Cauffman

McNeil Consumer Healthcare
Liberty Building
Fort Washington, Pennsylvania

If designing a contemporary office to stimulate interaction, collaborative effort and cross-functional teamwork is desirable, constructing the facility to use sustainable resources such as environmentally friendly materials, energy efficient fixtures and natural light enhances its value even further. That's why the new, two-floor, 52,000-square-foot office of McNeil Consumer Healthcare in Fort Washington, Pennsylvania, designed by Francis Cauffman, is so desirable for its 228 employees. A mixture of open workstations, internal private offices, large conference rooms, enclosed team rooms, touchdown areas, informal gathering places, hub coffee/bistro area, with wireless technology and ergonomic furnishings, support both collaborative and individual work. To maximize "visibility/accessibility" and "the use of natural light," the design places the open work areas along the building's perimeter and enclosed offices and meeting rooms in the interior. Not only does McNeil Consumer Healthcare gain a versatile workplace, the facility boasts USGBC LEED-Commercial Interiors Silver Certification for environmentally sustainable design. Sustainable elements include using products with high recycled content, natural light penetration and exterior views for 90 percent of the occupants, a 15 percent savings in annual energy costs, plus 75 percent of construction waste was diverted to uses other than landfill.

Top: Café.
Above: Team meeting room.
Left: General workspace.
Opposite: Quiet-touchdown room.
Photography: Don Pearse.

Francis Cauffman

Gebhardt & Smith, LLC
Baltimore, Maryland

Space is rightly treated as a precious commodity by today's law firms, and the new, one-floor, 20,000-square-foot Baltimore office of Gebhardt & Smith, designed by Francis Cauffman, represents an excellent example of how a substantial building program can fit comfortably within a modest floor area through creative design. Some 50 employees of a law firm established in 1975 to practice in such areas of law as business law, bankruptcy, banking law, commercial finance, real estate and civil litigation are housed in a facility encompassing private offices, conference center, library, support spaces, reception area and elevator lobby. The interiors are furnished to project an elegant, tailored and classic image with transitional furniture, a variety of lighting fixtures, and such timeless materials as wood, granite and glass. Every area is spacious, well lighted and effective. Why is there no sensation of high density or overcrowding? The design team credits comprehensive space planning and the incorporation of circulation paths as functional spaces wherever appropriate. Because such facilities as an open library and double-loaded filing corridors can accommodate both users and passersby, they free up what would otherwise be dedicated floor areas and shorten distances, saving space and time—another precious commodity in law practice.

Top left: Main conference room.
Top right: Reception.
Right: Office area.
Below right: Elevator lobby.
Photography: David Lamb.

Gensler

Atlanta	Houston	San Diego
Baltimore	La Crosse	San Francisco
Boston	Las Vegas	San Jose
Charlotte	London	San Ramon
Chicago	Los Angeles	Seattle
Costa Rica	Morristown	Shanghai
Dallas	New York	Tampa
Denver	Newport Beach	Tokyo
Detroit	Northern Virginia	Washington, DC
Dubai	Phoenix	

Gensler

Gensler

The London Stock Exchange
London, U.K.

Over three centuries old, the London Stock Exchange looks and behaves like a much younger enterprise after relocating from the City of London, London's financial district, to a new building at Paternoster Square, next to St Paul's Cathedral. Why? The Exchange traded a heavily compartmented and inward-looking 1960s facility for a 95 percent open and highly flexible modern environment, designed by Gensler, where 140,000 square feet of facilities on floors 1, 2, 3 and 7 plus ground floor and lower ground floor help 500 employees perform their tasks, inspire people to do business with the Exchange, and increase collaboration among business units. Its Media Centre, for example, functions as the Exchange's public face with multimedia facilities, radio booths, broadcasting studios, 120-seat auditorium, presentation suites and syndicate rooms. On typical office floors, open-plan workstations arrayed like trading desks encircle a central elliptical Hub for formal and ad hoc meetings overlooking the building's atrium. The Foundation café, the 70-seat main dining area, is a popular rendezvous for staff and clients. Praising the new facility, Exchange chairman Christopher Gibson-Smith points out, "Its design allows us to work in new ways and gives us the flexibility to continue our development as a commercial enterprise."

Clockwise from top left: Broadcast control room, conference room, workplace rows, the Hub, dining room, theater.

Opposite: Interior view from atrium.

Photography: Marcus Peel, Timothy Soar.

Gensler

Sidley Austin LLP
Chicago, Illinois

Above: Breakout area.
Right: Reception.
Below right: Boardroom.
Bottom right: Cafeteria.
Opposite: View of reception from elevator lobby.
Photography: Nick Merrick/ Hedrich Blessing.

Is traditional symbolism yielding to dynamic functionality in law offices? Consider the new award-winning 22-floor, 600,000-square-foot Chicago headquarters of Sidley Austin, a firm with over 1,700 lawyers in 16 offices worldwide. Sidley's largest office has been designed by Gensler, with whom it enjoys a long-term relationship, to house some 1,300 employees in a modern "inside out" environment featuring a universal design template on attorney floors that lets practice groups change floor plans with minimal disruption. Comprising such spaces as reception areas, private offices, open workstations, a conference center and mail/support room, the headquarters follows a stacking plan that consolidates support functions on lower floors, provides attorney floors with standardized office modules and furnishings and large, flexible interior workrooms, and creates a multiple-floor, state-of-the-art conference center joined by interconnecting stairs. Yet practicality does not preclude style and comfort. Subtle surprises emerge such as a fireplace or colorful curtains in interiors appointed in wood, stone, stainless steel, patterned glass, carpet, and classic modern furnishings. Materials in the building's public spaces appear here as well, acknowledging Sidley as a major tenant. Says an appreciative Michael Prapuolenis, Sidley's director of administration, "Gensler's expertise and familiarity with our firm culture are invaluable."

Gensler

Cole & Weber United
Seattle, Washington

Like other successful advertising agencies whose workplaces uniquely identify them, Cole & Weber United, a Seattle firm founded in 1931 that is part of WPP's voluntary global confederation of creative agencies, recently completed a new office that turns heads in an understated, Pacific Northwest way. The 6th-floor, 21,600-square-foot penthouse, designed by Gensler, includes private offices, open work areas, war rooms, team areas, sunken lounge space, pantry, editing room, focus room, conference room, copy/mail, and storage, along with a 5th-floor reception/lobby shared with four other companies through an

innovative floor plan also designed by Gensler. Cole & Weber's workplace stresses collaboration at every turn, with open workstations lining the perimeter and enclosed and support areas occupying the interior. Visitors won't mistake it for anywhere else, thanks to a design that boldly juxtaposes raw and natural elements such as concrete base building walls, concrete tile raised floors, and cedar plank walls against refined architectural elements featuring glass walls, sheer drapes, and iconic modern furnishings. Besides such details, what visitors see first is a sunken lounge where a pool table, large screen tv, and video games make it

resemble a comforting retro living room. In short, a great place to work with a "wow" factor.

Top right: Pantry.
Above middle right: Lobby.
Above right: Conference room.
Right: Sunken lounge.
Opposite: Hallway.
Photography: Sherman Takata/Gensler.

Gensler

Nihon L'Oréal
Tokyo, Japan

Though Nihon L'Oréal was established in Tokyo in 1996, well after the founding of L'Oréal in Paris in 1907, its parent has a long history in Japan. The French cosmetics giant first began selling products to Japanese beauty salons in 1964 and has prospered by developing new products in Japan specifically for Japanese consumers. Its sophisticated new, three-floor, 89,300-square-foot office, designed by Gensler, represents another company milestone, consolidating the staff of 13 brands previously scattered across multiple locations. The design represents a delicate balancing act, establishing a unified corporate awareness without discounting the identities of the 13 brands. To achieve this, the cafeteria, placed immediately behind the main reception area in the facility's brand-neutral shared zone, is treated as the main feature. This spacious espresso bar-style environment encourages encounters between employees to promote inter-brand communication, and is well-equipped and attractive enough for client presentations and major company functions. Elsewhere, private offices, open areas, and meeting rooms are carefully organized around the various brands. However, the design's common facilities, including the employee shop, library, make-up artists' studio, and merchandising room as well as the cafeteria, form its essence and jointly proclaim: Welcome to Nihon L'Oréal.

Top left: Reception.
Top right: Open break area.
Far left: Expresso bar-style cafeteria.
Left: Library seating booths.
Photography: Atsushi Naka-michi/Nacasa & Partners Inc.

H. Hendy Associates

4770 Campus Drive
Suite 100
Newport Beach, CA 92660
949.851.3080
949.851.0807 (Fax)
www.hhendy.com

H. Hendy Associates

H. Hendy Associates

The Impac Companies
Irvine, California

Major corporate relocations can mobilize hundreds of employees and consume hundreds of thousands of square feet. The consolidation of 700 employees of The Impac Companies from five buildings to one in Irvine, California stands out as a particularly successful move. The seven-floor, 204,000 square-foot facility which includes reception, café, private offices, boardroom, conference rooms, mail center and data center was designed by H. Hendy Associates. For Impac, a mortgage real estate investment trust, the project's overriding goal was to unify the staff. The winning build-to-suit scheme establishes an open, modular and classically modern environment focusing on activity hubs and a café. Developed by the design team in close cooperation with Impac, the space reflects the company's innovative, family-oriented culture and gives employees an effective workplace with flexibility to grow. The activity hubs not only provide

community spaces for copy, coffee break and conference areas, they act as wayfinding devices. The ImpaCafé offers employees deli-style food service in an informal setting of brick walls, white tile, mosaic flooring and wainscot paneling. Commenting on the facility, Impac's senior vice president of operations proudly notes that H. Hendy Associates "designed a space that feels as if our employees built it together."

Above: Boardroom.

Left: Elevator lobby.

Below left: Open office and hub area.

Below middle left: Cafeteria servery and cashier.

Bottom left: Cafeteria dining rooms.

Opposite: Reception.

Photography: Lawrence Anderson.

67

H. Hendy Associates

Birtcher Development & Investments
Irvine, California

Top: Private office.
Above left: Open office.
Above right: Executive office.
Right: Conference room.
Opposite: Virtual reception area.
Photography: Toshi Yoshimi.

Birtcher Development & Investments, a leading, privately held, West Coast real estate developer, and H. Hendy Associates, its interior designer, have transformed the penthouse space into a bright new facility with a California coastal feel. The design team retained existing assets such as entry doors directly off the elevator lobby, 11-foot ceilings, and a workable layout of private offices and built-in workstations. The reception area sets the tone by contrasting a neutral sand and ivory palette with dark chocolate wood; using such materials as marble, leather, and Venetian plaster to house what Birtcher calls a "virtual reception area." To create an open, well lit, contemporary environment the building shell was stripped of old traditional moulding and replaced with large bays of sandblasted glass windows at office fronts, layered with drywall and custom wood and glass doors. As a result, the open area is flooded with light and supplemented with indirect lighting. Designers refinished all workstations by applying a series of layers consisting of natural wallcovering, wood and stone. Everyone was thrilled with the transformation. Says Birtcher president and owner, " The finished product certainly exceeded my expectations."

H. Hendy Associates

Crevier Classic Car Company
Costa Mesa, California

Above: View from foyer to game room.

Top left: Showroom.

Far Left: Dining Room.

Left: Game Room.

Below left: Library/Lounge.

Photography: Lawrence Anderson.

California dreaming is often about cars. Owners of precious vintage and exotic automobiles in southern California could not have dreamed of a better venue to store, display and maintain their vehicles than the new Crevier Classic Car Company, in Costa Mesa, California. H. Hendy Associates designed the 28,000 square-foot state-of-the-art, museum-quality storage facility. This is the creative concept of its owner, Don Crevier, who also operates Crevier BMW in Santa Ana, one of the nation's top BMW dealerships. The challenge to H. Hendy Associates was to transform a conventional industrial warehouse into a sparkling destination "staffed by car enthusiasts for car enthusiasts" while meeting strict and complex regulations about car exhaust, fire safety, and building mechanical and electrical systems. Customers have full access to an elegant and inviting reception area highlighted by a raised, cove-lit ceiling element with evocative platinum and silver toned finishes in a pattern that is a nod to Crevier's BMW Dealership. There is also a game room with pool table and refreshment center, a library/lounge area stocked with numerous automotive periodicals, books and trophies, as well as a dining room and outdoor patio area. All spaces have large plasma screen televisions and wireless internet access. The design team has drawn inspiration from old Humphrey Bogart movies, Packard clubs, and the popular culture of the 1930s to produce a showroom where warm wood paneling and polished floors reflect the cars' lustrous paint finishes, classic posters for car advertisements adorn the walls, and vintage gas pumps stand like sculpture among the cars. The club features original artwork and luxurious and comfortable

H. Hendy Associates

transitional furnishings such as plush banquette seating and club chairs in colors and patterns evocative of the 1930s. The resulting design surrounds car owners and their guests in a perfect setting for car conversation and socializing. To quote the company's owner, "H. Hendy Associates' carefully crafted design elements evoke a refined energy and excitement that car aficionados know well. Coupled with added features like our experienced on-site technicians and museum quality storage showroom, the club is a virtual mecca for car enthusiasts."

Top left: View of game room showing bar.

Left: Close-up of showroom.

Huntsman Architectural Group

50 California Street
Seventh Floor
San Francisco, CA 94111
415.394.1212
415.394.1222 (Fax)
www.huntsmanag.com

48 Wall Street
Fourth Floor
New York, NY 10005
212.693.2700
212.693.2123 (Fax)

Huntsman Architectural Group

Huntsman Architectural Group

KKR Financial LLC
San Francisco, California

Relationships are vital to KKR Financial, a specialty finance investment company founded by Kohlberg Kravis Roberts & Co. and founding partners Saturnino Fanlo and David Netjes. Accordingly, its new, one-floor, 25,000-square-foot headquarters in San Francisco, designed by Huntsman Architectural Group, provides a casually elegant contemporary setting where 50 senior analysts, analysts and administrative personnel work and welcome clients. The space is shaped by its 50th floor location in the heart of the Financial District and by the CEO's preference for a five-star hotel's ambiance over a traditional business environment. To

exploit the incomparable views, private offices, guest lobby, conference rooms and other front-of-house functions line the perimeter, while workstations, trading floor, catering kitchen, pantry, restrooms and storage occupy the interior. Huntsman worked with Kate McIntyre of Ironies Inc., a furniture design studio, to develop "twig and leaf" furniture of wood and forged iron to establish a residential look, completing the effect with furnishings emphasizing natural materials and fine craftsmanship, plus pieces from a growing art collection. Busy as they are, employees notice their workplace. Notes Laurie Poggi, KKR's director of investor relations, "Of most importance, the space had to be rewarding to our professionals. Our new office reflects this."

Top: Reception and lobby.
Above: Private office.
Left: Conference room.
Opposite: Elevator lobby.
Photography: David Wakely.

Huntsman Architectural Group

Redwood Trust, Inc.
Mill Valley, California

A forward-thinking CEO, a linear building with good east-west exposure and serene exterior views, and a responsive design team have produced an unusually bright and spacious modern workplace for 54 employees of Redwood Trust, Inc., a real estate investment trust in Mill Valley, California. The one-floor, 20,000-square-foot facility, designed by Huntsman Architectural Group, has no private offices because the CEO believes the traditional office layout is too confining. To break up the expansive volume that runs along a 137-foot-long span with east-facing, 26-foot-high windows and an exposed truss ceiling, the office area features six- and eight-workstation clusters, staggered to create alternating setbacks for impromptu meetings and reading areas in front of the windows, as well as acoustic ceiling panels that reduce reverberation and diffuse overhead light. By contrast, the meeting area on the building's west side, containing the reception area, main conference room, guest lounge and hotelling center, is characterized by such differentiated spaces as the highly visible and centrally located glass enclosure of the main conference room. Speaking for her colleagues, Rosalyn Chan, vice president of Redwood Trust, says, "We would like to thank our architects for making our design and build-out project an entirely delightful experience."

Top left: Exterior of main conference room.
Top right: Reception desk.
Right: Conference room.
Opposite: Workstation area.
Photography: David Wakely.

Huntsman Architectural Group

Pixar Animation Studios
Pixar West Village
Emeryville, California

Fans of the animated feature films Toy Story, Finding Nemo, and The Incredibles might easily guess that Pixar Animation Studios, the Academy Award-winning computer animation studio behind these hits, works predominately in private offices. After all, audience members include many devotees of computer games and other high-tech media. The challenge in developing the new, one-floor, 56,000-square-foot Pixar West Village in Emeryville, California, designed by Huntsman Architectural Group, was to create areas where 102 employees could collaborate, and to restore the facility's L-shaped 1940s

brick warehouse in the spirit of the main building on Pixar's adjacent campus. Huntsman's scheme turns the transept into the "town square" for private offices, technical support space, story board rooms, computer support, video conferencing/conference areas, break room, mail room, lounge/interaction areas, yoga room and screening room. The revitalized space provides a neutral environment where offices have windows facing only broad interior "boulevards," shuffleboard or casual lounges enliven corridor intersections, minimal metal-and-glass enclosures house meeting spaces, and comfortable

modern furnishings complement the restored structure. Tom Carlisle, Pixar's facilities director, observes, "The character and charm of this 1940s warehouse space was restored and revitalized with a clean, elegant design to create an industrial yet warm working environment."

Above right: Plastic arts studio.
Right: Conference room.
Below: Employee lounge.
Opposite: Building lobby.
Photography: Sharon Risedorph.

Huntsman Architectural Group

Moody's KMV
San Francisco, California

Top left: Elevator lobby and guest lounge.

Top right: Private offices and open-plan workspace.

Left: Reception and guest lounge.

Photography: David Wakely.

Following the acquisition of KMV, a San Francisco-based credit-analysis provider, by Moody's, an established New York investment firm, the new office has been designed by Huntsman Architectural Group to integrate two different corporate cultures and accommodate future growth. The 58,300 square foot headquarters fills its sizable floorplate with an ambitious program for 270 employees, encompassing lobby, reception area, private and open offices, conference rooms, training room, information technology rooms, lounge areas, dining and recreation room, kitchen, and mail room. The headquarters fills its sizable floorplate with an ambitious program, encompassing lobby, reception area, private and open offices, conference rooms, training room, information technology rooms, lounge areas, dining and recreation room, kitchen, and mail room. To simplify wayfinding, the floor plan harnesses the building's atrium courtyard to let daylight penetrate deep inside, and groups departments around the atrium's "town square" spaces to form distinct zones with key office functions. Interiors rely on a coolly efficient glass and aluminum wall system to define space, but offset its geometry with such furnishings as gold-, cobalt- and coral-striped carpet, turquoise glass tile, walnut flooring, cherry wood benches, leather upholstered lounge chairs, and a 60-foot art wall, printed on a wall covering evoking the corporate logo. The design's impact is summed up by Daniell Moss, facilities manager for Moody's KMV, declaring, "It is such a privilege to work in an environment such as this."

KlingStubbins

2301 Chestnut Street
Philadelphia, PA 19103
215.569.2900
215.569.5963 (Fax)
www.klingstubbins.com

KlingStubbins

KlingStubbins

Brandywine Realty Trust
Corporate Headquarters
Radnor, Pennsylvania

It's true. Brandywine Realty Trust, one of America's largest full-service real estate companies and a real estate operating company organized as a real estate investment trust, hadn't initially planned to move its corporate headquarters to 555 East Lancaster Avenue in Radnor, Pennsylvania. However, as Brandywine executives monitored the renovation of the office building's entrance, lobby and atrium, an upgrade designed by KlingStubbins, they liked what they saw as a potential future-oriented image for the company. So what started as a property makeover quickly expanded to include a new, three-level, 53,000-square-foot headquarters office for some 165 employees. KlingStubbins had no time to lose, however. Since the design, construction and relocation were to be completed in just seven months, the design team conducted on-site programming and planning sessions, gathered data, conducted visioning workshops, and quickly developed a planning concept and design approach. Well aware that the upgrade of the building, which could be characterized as "expect the unexpected," had resulted in the more extensive assignment, KlingStubbins worked with Brandywine to challenge conventional thinking about office space. The results are visible at focal points

Left: Reception desk.

Far left: Lobby.

Opposite top left: Think tank.

Opposite top middle: Private offices and open workstations.

Opposite top right: Entry door.

Opposite bottom: Lobby.

Photography: Tom Crane Photography.

KlingStubbins

throughout the facility, from the terrazzo flooring and fireplace in the lobby to the pool table and pinball machine in the break room. Yet the surprises show up in task-oriented areas as well. The open workstations, for example, have low-height partitions and are slightly angled from the building grid within spaces that expose such building system components as ductwork, columns and cabling to celebrate the art and science of building construction. Private offices, delineated by all-glass walls and doors facing the corridors, appear to flow seamlessly into open areas, encouraging communication at all levels of the organization. Even the choice of furnishings provides evidence of fresh ideas, summoning rich materials and finishes to support the strong design concept. Of course, such high-profile areas as reception, conference rooms and training center receive a higher level of finish and detail than typical areas. Still, everywhere employees and visitors look, Brandywine Realty Trust demonstrates that a modern, effective and well-designed environment has a legitimate role to play in today's business world.

Above left: Connecting stair.
Above right: Break room.
Left: Huddle area.
Opposite: Atrium and spiral staircase.

KlingStubbins

Avery Dennison
Fasson Roll North America, NEO Facility
Mentor, Ohio

How does your staff work? Good relationships among employee groups and between employees and customers are essential to successful organizations, and the new, 0-story, 240,000-square-foot NEO Facility in Mentor, Ohio for 600 employees of Fasson Roll North America, part of Fortune 500 giant Avery Dennison, eloquently illustrates how workplaces can support them. At this location, Fasson Roll North America, which produces Fasson-brand pressure sensitive base materials, reflective and graphic materials and performance polymers, houses an office and research facility, designed by KlingStubbins, including a 45,000-square-foot laboratory, state-of-the-art pilot coater facility and conference/training center. Avery Dennison's three-fold design directive called for creating a modern facility for product research and pilot testing programs, facilitating corporate cultural changes to increase productivity and internal communications, and providing an environment to maximize customer partnering. To achieve these goals, a critical space known as the "Link" unites the research, testing and administrative functions by centralizing the main reception, informal meeting areas, private meeting rooms, customer product display, coffee bar, cafeteria and multi-function meeting room large enough for "town meetings" and community activities. Secured for employee interaction with customers, vendors and other visitors, the space maintains a distinctive atmosphere of hospitality insiders appreciate as much as outsiders.

Top left: Link.
Top right: Conference center.
Left: Elevator lobby screen.
Opposite top: Link seating with corporate timeline.
Opposite bottom left: Conference room.
Opposite bottom middle: Coffee bar with interconnecting stair.
Opposite bottom right: Cafeteria/coffee bar.
Photography: Tom Crane Photography.

KlingStubbins

BT Radianz
Boston, Massachusetts

Multi-national commerce is a fact of everyday life, so the new, one-level, 5,000-square-foot Boston office for 21 employees of British Telecom's BT Radianz subsidiary has been designed by KlingStubbins to blend a collegial, team-driven North American atmosphere with the European parent company's office planning standards, and to do so without cultural conflict. Globe hopping is commonplace for BT Radianz, a leading provider of secure, reliable, and scalable connectivity to the global financial community. The Boston facility blends pragmatism and sensitivity to maximize daylight penetration into the interior work areas by arraying all enclosed rooms, including private offices and conference rooms, along the periphery and installing glass and translucent resin wherever appropriate. However, the space also demonstrates the importance of design in shaping public perception. The circular reception area, which acts as a central organizer for the space, boldly reinforces BT Radianz's image as a dynamic, high-tech, and forward-thinking organization. That the facility is also enlivened by finishes with European precedents, such as sliding, barn-style glass doors, stainless steel, maple, and neutral colors with bold accents on selected walls, promotes the company's credibility as an organization where a global work force can excel.

Top left: Reception.
Top right: Conference room.
Above right: Lunchroom.
Right: Private offices and open workstations.
Photography: John Horner.

Leotta Designers Inc

601 Brickell Key Drive
Suite 602
Miami, FL 33131
305.371.4949
305.371.2844 (Fax)
www.leottadesigners.com

Leotta Designers Inc

Leotta Designers Inc

American Airlines Admirals Club
Miami International Airport
Miami, Florida

Miami is hailed as a gateway to the Americas, and the statistics logged at Miami International Airport amply support this claim. A total of 14.7 million international passengers and 1.68 million tons of international freight in 2006 place Miami International first in international freight and third in international passengers among U.S. airports. The city's strategic importance was certainly relevant when American Airlines held a design competition for its recently completed American Airlines Admirals Club at the airport's North Terminal (D Concourse) expansion, which called for a schematic design and palette indicative of Miami's look and feel. The winning submission for the two-floor, 31,000-square-foot facility for 500 guests and employees, designed by Leotta Designers, simultaneously provides a sleek, contemporary environment evoking the spirit of Miami's dynamic, multi-cultural community, and incorporates the special facilities that an Admirals Club requires. Indeed, the reception area, lounge, TV lounge, Business Center, bar, Quiet Way, music room, cyber café, children's center, VIP lounge, cappuccino bar, showers, kitchen and executive offices effectively promote the American Air-

lines brand while incorporating the natural colors and light unique to Miami and architectural motifs recalling its flamboyant past. However, the effortless flow of circulation and highly functional layout required considerable design ingenuity. The location of the Admirals Club placed it at a transitional node or "knuckle" of the new, mile-long North Terminal expansion. To resolve such problematic conditions in

Top right: TV lounge and cappuccino bar.
Right: Entry level reception.
Below: Bar.
Opposite: The Promenade.
Photography: Joseph Lapeyra.

Leotta Designers Inc

the then unfinished shell as angular forms, huge supports for an overhead rail system, and obstacles to extensive plumbing lines, the design team developed a unique "nautilus shell" plan that clustered all service facilities in the center to minimize plumbing costs, centralized food services to conceal them from guests, and created spiraling lounges and other facilities to exploit views of the tarmac and concourse rotunda. The huge support columns became design accents and the impetus for the long, curving spine, The Promenade, connecting such major facilities as the main lounge and the Business Center, placed immediately off reception for hurried travelers. Of course, none of this is obvious to the guest, who

is greeted on the arrival level by a dramatic, curvilinear stair wrapped with a 25-foot-high, polished stainless steel drape. As he or she ascends the stair, a wall of polished, stainless steel-framed fiber optic undulating glass waves shifts subtly from blue to green to the sound of New Age music, enthusiastically proclaiming, "Welcome to Miami!"

Left: Children's center.
Middle left: Grand stair chandelier from main lobby.
Bottom left: The Quiet Way.
Opposite: Main lobby.
Photography: Joseph Lapeyra.

Leotta Designers Inc

Stearns Weaver Miller Weissler Alhadeff & Sitterson, PA
Ft. Lauderdale, Florida

Top: Elevator lobby and reception.

Above: Library.

Opposite: Conference center.

Photography: Joseph Lapeyra.

A new, one-floor, 20,000-square-foot Ft. Lauderdale law office for 90 employees of Stearns Weaver Miller Weissler Alhadeff & Sitterson, designed by Leotta Designers, recently became an unusual test of the office design concepts and standards developed for refurbishing the firm's 90,000-square-foot head office in Miami. The reason: Although the two facilities were being designed simultaneously, the Ft. Lauderdale office was slightly ahead of its counterpart in Miami. This time lag presented a novel situation for the 115-attorney commercial law firm, which

counsels clients ranging from Fortune 500 companies to small businesses and entrepreneurs, and its design firm. The design concepts and standards, based on having two sizes of perimeter offices opposite paralegals and assistants, would have to be applied to a floor plate quite unlike the one faced by the head office. Fortunately, they proved flexible enough to produce a high quality environment for the reception area, conference center, law offices, war rooms, library and café in Ft. Lauderdale. War rooms, for example, were located immediately adjacent to the parale-

gals—opposite the attorneys for ease of access—while war room case files were strategically placed on either side and equipped with flexible tables for multiple team access. Concurrently, the library was reduced in size and treated as a linear accent space along a main access corridor, adjacent to the south reception area, to minimize the need for floor area. The conference center

Leotta Designers Inc

was centered around the north (main) reception area to maintain security by keeping visitors out of general office space. The resulting interior is contemporary in spirit, offering such timely features as a material palette of mahogany, anigre and maple wood, carpet, marble and porcelain tile, linen wallcoverings, and contemporary furniture. Additionally, there is a hip café positioned just off the center core, and an angled floor plan with hall vistas that focus on such "visual moments" as trellises. Given such fresh, light-filled and lively spaces, it's an appropriate setting for a firm as proud of its pro bono work for people unable to afford counsel and its dedication to community-based charitable organizations as it is of its corporate practice.

Top: Typical corridor with secretarial stations.
Left: Café.

96

Looney Ricks Kiss Architects, Inc.

175 Toyota Plaza
Suite 600
Memphis, TN 38103
901.521.1440
901.525.2760 (Fax)

209 10th Avenue South
Suite 408
Nashville, TN 37203
615.726.1110
615.726.1112 (Fax)

182 Nassau Street
Suite 201
Princeton, NJ 08542
609.683.3600
609.683.0054 (Fax)

671 Front Street
Suite 220
Celebration, FL 34747
407.566.2575
407.566.2576 (Fax)

31 Main Street
Rosemary Beach, FL 32461
850.231.6833
850.231.6838 (Fax)

5307 East Mockingbird Lane
Suite 220
Dallas, TX 75206
214.242.7650
214.242.7655 (Fax)

315 East Bay Street
Suite 400
Jacksonville, FL 32202
904.224.1046
904.224.1047 (Fax)

5615 Corporate Boulevard
Suite 100B
Baton Rouge, LA 70808
225.928.4905
225.928.4906 (Fax)

1414 Pearl Street
Suite 200
Boulder, CO 80302
303.440.1257
303.440.8918 (Fax)

www.lrk.com
info@lrk.com

Looney Ricks Kiss Architects, Inc.

First Horizon National Corporation Headquarters
Memphis, Tennessee

First Horizon National Corporation has come a long way since its predecessor, the First National Bank of Memphis, opened in 1864. Then, the city was reeling from the Civil War. Today, First Horizon National Corporation is one of America's top 30 bank holding companies. In a comprehensive renovation of the office building it erected in 1963, First Horizon asked Looney Ricks Kiss Architects, which has served them for the past 20 years, to design the award-winning renovation of its executive quarters, including five executive offices, executive dining room, and state-of-the-art boardroom atop its 23-story tower, and an open office area, private offices, executive conference room and courtyard atop its three-story, low-rise structure. The facility's new look combines classic modern architecture and a traditional scheme of perimeter offices and interior open work areas with timeless contemporary furnishings and advanced technology. One potential challenge, the low slab-to-slab height on the 23rd floor, led to the creative use of accessible acoustic ceiling panels that resemble drywall, eliminating the need for ordinary access panels. Combined with open slots in the ceiling that accommodate HVAC distribution, the panels give the impression of a limitless ceiling, a fitting image for First Horizon.

Top left: Boardroom.
Top right: Courtyard.
Upper right: Elevator lobby.
Above: Pre-function.
Right: Executive dining room.
Opposite: Reception.
Photography: Rick Bostick/ Photo Design Inc., Joe Aker/Aker Zvonkovic Photography.

Looney Ricks Kiss Architects, Inc.

Baker Donelson Bearman Caldwell & Berkowitz, PC
Memphis, Tennessee

After decades in an existing space, the Memphis office of Baker, Donelson, Bearman, Caldwell & Berkowitz, PC, one of America's 100 largest law firms, welcomed change. The firm wanted a more effective and economical workplace as well as a fresh appearance, and retained Looney Ricks Kiss Architects, designer of its existing space, to create a new six-floor, 100,000-square-foot office in the First Tennessee Build-

ing, a distinguished 1963 structure. Its new facility centralizes reception duties and conferencing on one floor, placing the reception area and main conference rooms on the west side to exploit spectacular Mississippi River views. Because the boardroom, pre-function room, reception area and library area are connected by oversized sliding doors to create one contiguous area, the floor also accommodates firm-

wide announcements, parties and dinners. Cooperation and collegiality are encouraged on other floors by locating legal secretaries adjacent to the attorneys they serve, lowering bookcases and file areas for impromptu meetings in perimeter corridors, and introducing a bright, open employee lounge for casual gatherings. Appraising the classic modern interior of timeless furnishings and iconic pieces, Rob Liddon, a shareholder of Baker, Donelson, Bearman, Caldwell & Berkowitz, lauds the "entirely fresh look and efficient work environment."

Right: Art installation.
Below: Boardroom.
Bottom left: Typical floor.
Bottom right: Pre-function.
Opposite top: Reception desk.
Opposite bottom: Reception.
Photography: Rick Bostick/ Photo Design Inc.

Looney Ricks Kiss Architects, Inc.

Looney Ricks Kiss Architects, Inc.
Jacksonville, Florida

A workplace is revealing, and no one knows this better than designers like Looney Ricks Kiss Architects, which recently developed a new, four-level, 12,500-square-foot office for 44 employees in a Jacksonville, Florida loft building. Established in 1983, the firm is now a 220-person architecture, planning, interiors, environmental graphics, and research firm headquartered in Memphis with offices in Tennessee, Texas, Florida, Louisiana, Colorado, and New Jersey. What makes the loft building so appropriate is the presence of original brick walls, high ceilings, large windows, and quality light. Believing that work is the central focus of its environment, and the open studio culture is key to its work, Looney Ricks Kiss Architects readily adapted the structure for the open, spare and refined spaces where its creative and collaborative activities thrive. Every facility, including reception, conference rooms, charrette areas, open studios, private offices, library, print room and kitchen, promotes collaborative work. Conference and charrette areas, for example, are separated by sliding glass doors, while multiple resource libraries double as meeting spaces, most walls are finished with magnetic white boards, tackable surfaces or glass for writing, furnishings are easy to move, and daylight and electric lighting blend seamlessly. As clients can see, it's a great place to work.

Top: Conference room.

Above left: Resource area.

Above: Reception/charrette.

Right: Charrette area.

Opposite bottom left: Open studio.

Opposite bottom right: Library.

Photography: Jack Gardner/Jack Gardner Photography.

Looney Ricks Kiss Architects, Inc.

FedExForum Suite
Memphis, Tennessee

Memphis is justifiably proud of FedExForum, the largest public building construction project in the city's history and the home of both the Memphis Grizzlies of the NBA and the Tigers basketball team of the University of Memphis. Not only was the arena completed on time and on budget, it has proved to be a good neighbor to the historic entertainment district surrounding it. For this reason, a client approached Looney Ricks Kiss Architects to design a sponsor suite to reflect the high-spirited atmosphere that characterizes FedExForum and its athletic and musical events, and to appeal to the traditional, conservative and personal taste of its executives, who would frequent the facility. Accordingly, the award-winning suite has been developed as a comfortably elegant setting, equipped with a bar, lounge and arena seating, to permit visitors to engage with the game or program as intensely as they prefer. The spatial organization of the suite is subtly defined by the orientation of furniture and other built-in elements, the ceiling design, and the choice of materials, finishes and furnishings, highlighted by full-raised paneling, traditional cabinetry and millwork, custom wool rug, and custom stainless steel and red crackle glass table. Clearly, the action starts here.

Mancini•Duffy

39 West 13th Street
New York, NY 10011
212.938.1260
800.298.0868
212.938.1267 (Fax)

New York
New Jersey
Connecticut
Washington DC
London UK

www.manciniduffy.com
info@manciniduffy.com

Mancini•Duffy

Wachovia Securities
New York, New York

America's third largest brokerage group, Wachovia Securities is a national firm and affiliate of Wachovia Corporation whose culture reflects regional firms from which it evolved. Demonstrating its sensitivity to New York, the firm recently opened its five-floor, 176,500-square-foot, Manhattan facility, designed by Mancini•Duffy, in Mies van der Rohe's iconic Seagram Building (1958). The building's landmark status imposed challenges well beyond the requirements of a state-of-the-art work-

place for 1,130 employees. Due to the curtain wall's transparency, every interior element visible from outside had to meet the Landmarks Preservation Commission's stringent standards. Examples included the identical replacement of Seagram's distinctive luminous ceilings after ductwork was installed for an extensive HVAC system, the installation of the system's new generators and chillers, which could not be seen from street-level, and the decreasing height of raised floors on three trading

floors with 600 desks— again, acknowledging the luminous ceiling—by eliminating CPUs in favor of blade servers in "super IDF" rooms, centralizing most of the heat load. The monolithic interior design, featuring reception, client conference center, offices, conference rooms and interconnecting stair in addition to trading rooms, completes the setting with perimeter office glass fronts, wood veneers, white lacquer and modern furnishings, including furniture designed by Mies himself.

Clockwise from top left: Reception, conference room, typical work station, trading floor, interconnecting stair.

Opposite: Corridor into workspace with branding elements.

Photography: Peter Paige Photography.

Mancini•Duffy

Capital One
Headquarters
McLean, Virginia

Growing companies seeking facilities designed for change can learn much from the recent renovation and expansion of Capital One's 2,000-person, 14-floor, 490,000-square-foot headquarters in McLean, Virginia. Established in 1995, Capital One, a financial services company serving customers in the United States, United Kingdom and Canada, has become a Fortune 200 company in less than a decade. The project's objective has been to help the existing headquarters support projected growth, reflect corporate culture and facilitate business models. One major program element, the Future of Work, transforms office floors into non-hierarchical spaces that eliminate most enclosed offices in favor of open teaming areas and an open desking system. In the new conference center and atrium

designed by Mancini•Duffy, another key component features a 450-seat lecture hall that can convert into a smaller venue. In addition, the retail replan creates a new, two-story, street-like main entry lobby linking the entry, garage, security area, elevator core and conference center with such amenities as a Capital One Bank branch, fitness center, coffee shop and concierge services. Praising the outcome, Barry Mark, group manager of Capital One Services, Corporate Real Estate, says, "We have found Mancini•Duffy to be consistently attentive to our design concerns, our budgets and our schedules."

Clockwise from top left: Coat check desk in atrium, second floor lecture hall break areas facing atrium, typical office space, lecture hall.

Opposite: Atrium showing wall scrim before conference rooms.

Photography: Mark Ballogg/ Ballogg Photography, Inc.

Mancini•Duffy

Hughes Hubbard & Reed LLP
Charles Evans Hughes Conference Center
New York, New York

Top right: Corridor.

Right: Entry and signage.

Opposite top left: Conference room.

Opposite top right: Multipurpose room.

Opposite: Reception seating.

Photography: Peter Paige Photography.

Pride in a distinguished history dating from 1888 has never kept Hughes Hubbard & Reed LLP, a law firm recognized among "the profession's top tier" in a 2006 survey by *The American Lawyer* magazine, from embracing new ideas. One timely example is the state-of-the-art Charles Evans Hughes Conference Center that Hughes Hubbard recently completed as part of a new, one-floor, 24,000-square-foot space in New York that includes a reception area, offices for some 22 lawyers and staff,

five war rooms, multipurpose room and warming pantry, all designed by Mancini•Duffy. Named for the firm's founder and a chief justice of the Supreme Court, the Center serves wide-ranging needs with two large conference rooms, seating 150 and 250 people, and 10 smaller conference rooms, holding from four to 20. Yet the facility is as attractive and supportive as it is efficient and up-to-date. Its interior of stone, wood, carpet, glass, comfortable transitional furnishings, and sophisticated lighting will certainly help members

of a law firm with some 330 lawyers in offices in New York, Washington, D.C., Los Angeles, Miami, Jersey City, Paris and Tokyo—and a reputation as one of the finest litigation practices in the nation—to do their best.

Mancini•Duffy

SportsNet New York
New York, New York

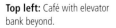

Top left: Café with elevator bank beyond.

Top right: Café.

Right: Open-plan administrative area.

Bottom right: Reception.

Photography: Peter Paige Photography.

If you're operating a popular sports cable network in New York City owned by the New York Mets, Time Warner, and Comcast, and you need a workplace for 60 employees that projects an image of modernity, light and energy, what would you do? The response can be viewed in the new, two-floor, 24,500-square-foot office of SportsNet New York, designed by Mancini•Duffy. Every facility provided, from the reception area, executive offices, and open-plan administrative offices to the interconnecting stair, café and pantry, is part of a finely crafted composition of glass walls, walnut pivot doors, circular light fixtures and horizontal and vertical lumi-

nous planes, counteracting limited daylight transmitted from the building's small, punched windows and low ceilings. It's a crisply detailed setting, employing such materials as wood, stainless steel, glass, leather, metallic textile sheers, carpet, and contemporary furnishings in a white, brown and orange color palette to encourage employees to gather and work together at communal facilities, clustered at the entry point from the elevator lobby and stacked vertically at the stair, when they're not at their individual work stations. Simultaneously comfortable and invigorating, the design aptly reinforces the network's slogan, "The Home of All Things NY Sports."

Margulies & Associates

234 Congress Street
Sixth Floor
Boston, MA 02110
617.482.3232
617.482.0374 (Fax)
www.margulies.com

Margulies & Associates

Carat Fusion
Boston, Massachusetts

Numerous creative steps paved the way to the dynamic environment for Carat Fusion's new, one-floor, 28,000-square-foot Boston office. Comprising private offices, open workspaces, conference rooms, meeting areas, reception area, showroom and break room—the space houses the 101 employees of this innovative marketing agency. Carat's staff are experts in creating the perfect image for their own clients; designer Margulies & Associates was challenged to produce the architectural equivalent in Back Bay's venerable John Hancock building. Inspired by Carat's logo design—a spinning, multi-colored sphere that represents the dynamism of their interactive work—and using 3D design tools to illustrate design concepts, Margulies & Associates guided its client through the design process. The final scheme takes advantage of the building's narrow floorplate to provide daylight and spectacular views for all. Such features as a striking lobby and reception area, full-glass office fronts, contemporary furnishings that include signature pieces in conspicuous areas, and sophisticated lighting that combines daylight with energy-efficient electric sources give the workplace its open, youthful atmosphere. Steve Andrews, Carat Fusion's CFO, recently praised Margulies & Associates for "hands-on involvement and resourcefulness from day one."

Margulies & Associates

OneBeacon Insurance
Canton, Massachusetts

Right: "Spring"-themed conference room.

Below: Indoor park and water feature.

Bottom: Individual gathering places.

Opposite: Water feature.

Photography: Warren Patterson.

Imagine holding your next meeting at a gazebo, terrace or fountain. They're some of the options awaiting 1,200 employees at the distinctive headquarters of OneBeacon Insurance in Canton, a Boston suburb. To consolidate personnel from downtown Boston and suburban Foxboro in one central location, the company recently converted an existing structure into a new, two-floor, 280,000-square-foot headquarters, designed by Margulies & Associates. It's a progressive workspace that offers a sense of community and features a lush, indoor year-round garden. Because OneBeacon, an organization founded in 1831 that sells

insurance through a network of independent agents, attributes its success to open communications among all groups, the workplace also features a non-hierarchical environment with no private offices and a generous number of conference rooms. The garden, designed by noted landscape architect Nelson Hammer, RLA, combines a water feature, dense plantings, outdoor furniture and landscaping materials. The design succeeds in transforming an unappealing existing courtyard into an interior urban park of individual outdoor and indoor areas where employees can eat lunch, relax and conduct

business. Conveying the company's satisfaction with its new home, John Ferrari, vice president-real estate, says, "The interior courtyard has already proven itself to be an effective and versatile space."

Margulies & Associates

Major Insurance Company
Member Services Center
Quincy, Massachusetts

As a health care organization, this Major Insurance Company recognizes the importance of an individual's work environment on his or her health. When the company purchased and renovated an early 1980s, seven-floor, 345,000-square-foot office building in Quincy, Massachusetts for its new Member Services Center, it gained its first opportunity in more than 30 years of leasing to fully manage the development of a major workplace for 1,500 employees. Designed by Margulies & Associates, the result has been an exceptionally healthy and functional environment providing physical comfort, energy efficiency, handicap accessibility, updated technology, easier parking and better food service. In fact, the new private offices, open workstation areas, cafeteria with full-service kitchen, on-site childcare center, and 1,350-car parking garage represent not only a major improvement over the existing premises, but also a LEED-certified workplace. The indoor air quality is excellent, most occupants enjoy exterior views and daylight, efficient design and operations will save some $110,000 annually in energy costs, and materials and furnishings are environmentally-friendly. Even the original, seven-story atrium has been improved, changing one awkward and uninviting void into three attractive social spaces: a three-story entry hall and two two-story gathering places on floors four and six. Advocates of green design take note.

Above left: Atrium from above.

Above: Cafeteria.

Right: Atrium at entrance.

Opposite top left: Gathering place with pivoting panels.

Opposite top right: Daycare facility.

Opposite middle right: Wheelchair accessible kitchenette.

Photography: Warren Patterson.

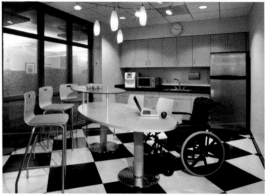

Margulies & Associates

National Development
Newton Lower Falls, Massachusetts

What happens when a real estate developer becomes its own client? One particularly inspired ending to this timeless story is the new, two-story, 20,000-square foot renovation of the headquarters for National Development, a company in historic Newton Lower Falls, Massachusetts that has produced over 12 million square feet of construction throughout New England since 1983. National Development retained

Margulies & Associates to establish a new look that would simultaneously reflect the firm's work as a developer, contractor, investor and asset manager, respect the community's heritage, and improve office operations. The "edgy but functional" design celebrates what National Development does best by expressing the imaginative thinking and quality materials and workmanship that characterize its real

estate projects. Among the highlights of the private offices, open office areas, reception, conference rooms, and support spaces, are the location of client-centered space at the front of the office, minimizing travel by clients and visitors, informal shared staff spaces that provide respite during work and relaxation after-hours, and contemporary furnishings that offer comfort without excessive formality. The improvements are

certainly not lost on National Development, where managing partner Ted Tye remarks, "I have heard many positive comments about the supportive design features."

Top left: Conference room.
Top right: Employee café.
Below: Reception area.
Photography: Warren Patterson.

Meyer Design, Inc.

227 E. Lancaster Avenue
Ardmore, PA 19003
610.649.8500
610.649.8509 (Fax)
www.meyerdesigninc.com
info@meyerdesigninc.com

Meyer Design, Inc.

Meyer Design, Inc.

Ardmore Partners
Radnor, Pennsylvania

A classic problem in office design has received a classic design solution at the new, one-floor, 5,000-square-foot office of Ardmore Partners, an investment company, in Radnor, Pennsylvania. The modern, efficient and attractive facility, designed by Meyer Design, provides 10 employees a reception area, private offices, open office area, conference rooms, an entertainment lounge/seating area, and a kitchen in an environment that seems more spacious and open than it actually is. To "open up" this compact volume, the design team has exposed the ceiling to accentuate its height, wrapped glass around private offices and conference rooms to promote visibility, and installed a variety of lighting sources, including standard 2-foot x 2-foot ceiling fixtures, direct/indirect pendant fixtures, and recessed fixtures set into walls, to introduce light in a naturalistic way that adds detail and variety. Of course, since glass enclosures make privacy a potential issue, conference rooms are equipped with manually operated roller blinds. But Ardmore Partners has no reservations about its new home, which easily accommodates social events in the entertainment lounge/seating area, and even gives its CEO and CFO the opportunity to indulge their passion for golf with two small depressions drilled into the floor slab for putting practice.

Top: Reception.

Left: View of conference room and kitchen from private office.

Opposite: Entertainment lounge/seating area.

Photography: Don Pearse.

Meyer Design, Inc.

Attalus Capital
Philadelphia, Pennsylvania

Location, location, location still matters in the Internet era. When Attalus Capital, an employee-owned investment management firm creating and actively managing portfolios of hedge funds for institutional investors, decided to vacate its suburban Philadelphia office for a new headquarters at the Cira Centre, a recently finished showcase property in Center City, it asked Meyer Design for a one-floor, 12,300-square-foot workplace with an unequivocal "wow" image. Visitors instantly perceive the excitement that energizes a facility comprising a reception area, private offices, open plan area, conference rooms, data room, file room and lunchroom. To capture and maximize breathtaking views of downtown Philadelphia from the building's full-height windows, the design places private offices with glazed fronts in interior space, giving all 20 staff members unimpeded sightlines. The drama is heightened by a design that brands the

Above: Reception area.

Right: Open plan area with view of Philadelphia.

Opposite top: Office of CEO.

Photography: Don Pearse.

space and helps build trust. While an architecture of rounded shapes derived from the company's logo contrasts with the Cira Centre's angular geometry to assert the Attalus "brand," patterned carpet directs the flow of traffic, and such quality materials as hardwood veneers, travertine, marble, hardwood floors, glass and faux leather floor tiles surround office occupants in a classic and supportive environment where "wow" has its place.

Meyer Design, Inc.

WXPN 88.5
Philadelphia, Pennsylvania

Left: Reception area.
Bottom: Open plan office area.
Opposite: Broadcast studios.
Photography: Don Pearse.

Listeners to WXPN 88.5, the National Public Radio station of the University of Pennsylvania, probably imagine its new, one-floor, 12,700-square-foot headquarters in Philadelphia's Hajoca Building to be as colorful and energetic as WXPN itself, and they wouldn't be disappointed. The thoughtfully detailed space, designed by Meyer Design for 70 workers with employee office spaces, student work study spaces, conference rooms, a lunchroom and four broadcast studios, retains much of the historic structure's character, including exposed trusses, exposed brickwork, and cathedral ceilings. As a broadcast studio, however, it incorporates such special provisions as triple-thick walls, three kinds of flooring, and durable finishes and furnishings to withstand the wear and tear of band equipment being moved in and out of the studio, as well as an elevator to convey artists to the studio—a far cry from the three flights of stairs they climbed with their gear at the old location. Of course, the design also visibly embodies the character of WXPN, which former general manager Vinnie Curran likened to a 1968 Volkswagen Beetle: young, hip but not too slick, and accessible to all. Roger LaMay, current general manager, cheerfully concludes, "It's a great balance between state-of-the-art and eclectic."

Meyer Design, Inc.

Capmark Finance, Inc.
Horsham, Pennsylvania

Like families on the move, organizations face numerous uncertainties when they exchange one environment for another. Fortunately, careful planning and design can resolve potential workplace issues in advance—as demonstrated by an appealing new, one-floor, 160,000-square-foot office in Horsham, Pennsylvania, designed by Meyer Design for Capmark Finance, a leading real estate financial company formerly known as GMAC Commercial Mortgage. The crisply tailored facility for 879 employees consists of a reception area, private offices, specialty trading floor, workstations, conference rooms, pantry and lunchroom. Its utilitarian yet inviting modern image resolves numerous potential challenges with seemingly effortless ease. Not only does it create the feeling of an urban trading floor to ease the transition to a suburban environment, it establishes an open environment where separate departments are subtly branded by finishes and furnishings. It adds visual interest through stainless steel, black granite and hardwood accents, and compensates for minimal daylight and extended proportions with glass-fronted interior private offices—essential for direct contact between managers and the trading floor. Additionally it shortens perspectives and promotes wayfinding via curving walls, columns, ceiling planes and soffits, and mimics daylight with a sophisticated lighting scheme. Built lean and fit with a touch of class, this business machine is ready for action.

Top left: Reception area with view of trading floor.
Top right: Conference room.
Left: Trading floor.
Photography: Don Pearse.

Mojo•Stumer Associates, P.C.

14 Plaza Road
Greenvale, NY 11548
516.625.3344
516.625.3418 (Fax)
www.MOJOSTUMER.com

Mojo•Stumer Associates, P.C.

McCance Medical Group
New York, New York

Patients visiting the Park Avenue office of McCance Medical Group in New York City, where Dr. Sean E. McCance maintains his practice as an orthopedic and spine surgeon, enter an interior environment that is reassuringly professional, secure and calm at the same time. The one-floor, 4,000-square-foot medical suite, designed by Mojo•Stumer Associates to incorporate a reception area, waiting room, consultation rooms, treatment rooms, office manager's office and billing office, is exactly what the doctor ordered. Currently co-director of Orthopedic Spine Surgery at Mount Sinai Medical Center and an attending spine surgeon at Lenox Hill Hospital, both Manhattan institutions, Dr. McCance sought a facility that would acknowledge his preference for a clear circulation path from front to back, daylight that could penetrate deep into interior areas, and functional space with exacting details to evoke the precision of his work, fine materials to establish an image of quality, and comfortable furnishings to put patients at ease. The interplay of materials and forms in the completed construction is particularly striking. A maple reception desk, for example, floats weightlessly on a stone plinth above a light stone floor. Elsewhere, a freestanding column is

Top: Doorway of private office.
Right: Private office.
Opposite: Corridor.
Photography: Tim Wilkes.

130

Mojo•Stumer Associates, P.C.

Above: Reception desk in profile.

Right: Reception area.

treated as sculpture with a cladding of stone and bronze, floating soffits serve to layer and accentuate ceiling height, and a translucent screen of vertically ribbed glass, bronze and maple encloses the doctors' offices and waiting room, separating private space from public space while transmitting sunlight to the waiting room and other windowless places. In assessing the new facility, Dr. McCance recently noted, "We accomplished what we set out to do. It works well and it looks great."

Mojo•Stumer Associates, P.C.

Birchwood Atrium Building
Jericho, New York

Prospective tenants can choose from many desirable low-rise office buildings in Jericho, New York, a hamlet of some 13,000 residents on Long Island, 27 miles east of New York City. As a result, the local office space market is quite competitive, with newer construction readily attracting tenants willing to pay top rents for modern accommodations. How do older properties compete? Remodeling can make a profound difference, as demonstrated by the Birchwood Atrium Building, a two-floor, 25,000-square-foot facility completed in 1985. To raise rents to levels enjoyed by newer and higher quality properties, Mojo•Stumer Associates was asked to return the existing public space, including the lobby, mailroom, and reception/security desk, to its original quality without altering its basic shell,

Right: Reception desk.
Bottom: Elevator.
Opposite: Entrance.
Photography: Mark Stumer, AIA.

134

Mojo•Stumer Associates, P.C.

greenhouse structure and staircase. Gutting all wall surfaces, the design team has introduced more up-to-date materials and forms, adding new, multi-level soffits to the plain ceiling, inserting wall planes accented in black steel and wood paneling, and replacing existing railings with contemporary ones. The dynamic, award-winning design has prompted the client to say, "There is no one in this building who will not appreciate this, even if I raise their rents now." Equally satisfying, the building is fully rented.

Top: Stairway.
Right: Mailboxes.

NELSON

The NELSON Building
222-30 Walnut Street
Philadelphia, PA 19106
215.925.6562
215.925.9151 (Fax)
www.nelsononline.com

NELSON

NELSON

Financial Institution
New York, New York

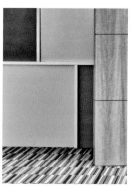

The assignment from a top financial institution to NELSON: Design new facilities for employees in landmark New York buildings. The challenge: Work within the guidelines of the client's corporate standards, upgrade finishes and furnishings, resolve existing on-site problems, and complete the assignment quickly and on budget. The result: The installations are up and running successfully. Making them possible is the long-running relationship between NELSON and the financial institution. The design firm has provided tactical planning, standards-based design and construction administration in support of the client's real estate strategic plan and ongoing capital improvements programs for over a dozen years. For a trading floor at one location, the contemporary design uses color panels to define the main circulation path and ceiling pop-ups to dramatize ceiling height, energizing the large floor plate for 450 traders. For 105 brokers and support staff at a second location, NELSON developed the client's largest premier banking facility nationwide, incorporating enhanced standards to help attract and retain employees in the competitive New York market. Mission accomplished!

Top left: Elevator lobby.
Top right: Toilet.
Above: Millwork detail.
Opposite: Trading room.
Opposite bottom left: Café.
Opposite bottom right: Conference room doorway.
Photography: Imagic.

NELSON

Towers Perrin
Minneapolis, Minnesota

Achieving greater efficiency in the work environment is a recurring goal for many organizations. The challenge is to do it without sacrificing quality or amenities. As demonstrated by the new, one-floor, 12,125-square-foot Towers Perrin office in Minneapolis, designed by NELSON, an efficient and effective space can actually improve the workplace. The facility for 53 employees of the respected global professional services firm is a study in balance and symmetry. The design, which embraces new universal corporate space standards, uses uncluttered lines to create an ambiance that is surprisingly open, light, airy and welcoming. To create this perception in a relatively dense environment, the design minimizes the use of full-height walls to reduce daylight obstruction from exterior windows, and incorporates 48 inch high systems furniture panels that are lower than the typical cube farm. Private offices are pulled off the building perimeter to the

building core and employ full-height glass fronts with glass sliding doors. Walls and systems furniture panels are light in color in contrast to bold color accent walls; natural maple and dark cherry veneer millwork add further interest. Sophisticated lighting provides both increased foot candles and sparkle in private offices, conference rooms and internal work areas. Among the details completing the effect are the reception area with outside views, a semi-enclosed employee break room that eliminates one wall to share the adjacent corridor space, and large plasma monitors utilizing technology to reinforce branding, hospitality and teamwork in the reception area and conference rooms. Towers Perrin employees and customers regard the relocation as an upgrade!

Below left: Conference room.
Below right: Reception.
Bottom right: Waiting area.
Photography: Phillip Prowse.

NELSON

Baxter International
Deerfield, Illinois

Design can be a powerful tool for businesses that know how to use it. To refresh its brand and bring a more high-tech, cutting-edge feel to its facilities in Deerfield, Illinois, Baxter International, a global healthcare company that assists healthcare professionals and their patients with treatment of complex medical conditions including hemophilia, immune disorders, kidney disease, cancer, trauma and other conditions, recently invited NELSON to renovate the headquarters building's 14,480-square-foot lobby space. NELSON contributed to the strategic rebranding, initiated as part of Baxter's 75th anniversary celebration, by designing a fresh new entrance for the 1970s building, introducing contemporary furniture and finishes, creating flexible spaces that can accommodate multiple functions for employees, visitors and the community, and working with MICE, an exhibit contractor, to design an interactive display area that totally

immerses visitors in Baxter's history and future as a leading source of medical devices, pharmaceuticals and biotechnology. The space provides an open environment that visitors can engage at will for education and inspiration. Using clean contemporary lines, such quality materials as maple millwork, carpet tile, porcelain tile, solid surfacing, blue glass—embodying the signature Baxter blue—metal, paint and fabric wrapped panels, along with dramatic lighting and examples of classic, modern furniture, the design produces a "wow" factor that is unmistakable. The effort has not gone unnoticed. Baxter's senior management, investors and visitors have all commented that the redesigned lobby has exceeded expectations and casts the company's future in a highly favorable light.

Top: Stair.
Above left: Interactive display.
Above right: Lobby seating.

OWP/P

111 West Washington Street
Suite 2100
Chicago, IL 60602-2714
312.332.9600
312.332.9601 (Fax)
www.owpp.com

Restoration Place
829 North First Avenue
Phoenix, AZ 85003-1401
602.294.6500
602.294.6565 (Fax)

OWP/P

Orbitz
Corporate Headquarters
Chicago, Illinois

How does a leading online business accommodate soaring customer demand? With over 19 million registered users, Orbitz, one of the top three online travel agencies, needed a new workplace immediately for over 1,000 employees. Fortunately, Orbitz's new, three-floor, 141,000-square-foot corporate headquarters in Chicago, designed by OWP/P, required just seven months, thanks to a highly coordinated building team. Subsequently, its lobby, private offices, open workstations, conference space, lunch room, break room and mothers' room are functional, responsive and branded as part of the

Orbitz experience with a distinctive personality. The large floorplates stay open by clustering private offices and teaming rooms around the core, establishing wide circulation runways for unobstructed window views and daylight, and providing bright contemporary furnishings that encourage social interaction. What distinguishes the facility, however, is a design scheme contrasting clean lines and polished finishes with rough materials and exposed building systems, reflecting the duality of technology and travel that defines Orbitz's success. The visual imagery is exciting, prompting Kathy Andreasen, Orbitz's senior

vice president, human resources and corporate administration, to comment, "Our leaders and employees love the new space, and it has been a huge boost for our business and our culture."

Top left: Corridor.
Top right: Informal conference area.
Above right: Open workstations.
Right: Break area.
Opposite: Lobby and corridor.
Photography: Steve Hall/ Hedrich Blessing.

OWP/P

Transswestern Commercial Services Regional Office
Chicago, Illinois

Top right: Breakout area.

Right: Behind-the-screen view of reception seating.

Bottom right: Conference room.

Opposite top: Reception.

Opposite bottom right: Break room.

Photography: Chris Barrett/ Hedrich Blessing.

To understand how good looks—or curb appeal in real estate parlance—help create a favorable public image, just visit the new Chicago office of Transswestern Commercial Services, a privately held national commercial real estate firm. The company has shrewdly used the aesthetics of its new, LEED Certified 21,000-square-foot facility, designed by OWP/P, in establishing a presence in the commercial real estate market where modern American architecture was born. Its configuration places communal areas such as the reception area and conference rooms up front, with full-height windows providing a strong visual identity and connection to the city beyond. The space offers a lively ambiance and spatial orientation, and integrates private offices for real estate professionals, who need privacy for heads-down work as well as interior areas for administrative staff and a multi-purpose open conference area and café. The use of glass interior walls for conference rooms, and private offices, innovative finishes, modern custom-designed furnishings and subtle architectural gestures throughout the facility that translate light, shadows and reflections of the buildings beyond and connect with the Windy City's legendary energy and iconic architecture.

OWP/P

OfficeMax
Corporate Headquarters
Naperville, Illinois

Top: Conference room.
Left: Reception.
Opposite: Atrium.
Photography: Jeff Millies/ Hedrich Blessing (top and opposite); Chris Barrett/ Hedrich Blessing (left and following page).

Chances are more than a few binders, paper clips, pens and other basic items in the typical U.S. workplace arrived at their final destination via OfficeMax. It is one of the nation's top three office supply businesses, a company that distributes some 10,000 name-brand and OfficeMax-branded products through direct sales, catalogs, the Internet and 935 superstores. It's a monumental scale of operations that became personally meaningful to some 1,500 OfficeMax employees during their recent move into a new, five-story (plus lower level), 350,000-square-foot corporate headquarters in Naperville, Illinois, designed by OWP/P. Efficiency and building a singular OfficeMax culture were key factors in the company's decision to relocate and consolidate employees in the new facility. OWP/P completed the complicated programming services needed to facilitate the consolidation and assisted in the planning and analysis of potential buildings, in addition to providing interior design and MEP engineering for the project. The design of the new headquarters has given the company a special opportunity to enhance its

OWP/P

already strong corporate brand, starting with the building's existing central atrium, which is large enough to hold gatherings of all the employees The design reemphasizes the company message of a single unified culture by applying abstract metaphors of office products that connect: rubber bands and paper clips. The workplace on the upper five levels remain bright thanks to open plan workstations and conference spaces enclosed in clear and translucent glass. Bright colors evoke the spirit of retail sales, help orient people in the workplace and provide energy in crisp, modern surroundings. On the lower level, custom carpeting serves as a vibrant canvas for the the full-service cafeteria and servery. Custom-designed fixtures —perceived as undulating

bands of light—illuminate these lively gathering places. The comprehensive effort incorporates key corporate values of passion, innovation and fun in the final results drawing favorable responses. Speaking for her colleagues, Carol Moerdyk, a senior vice president of OfficeMax, notes, "The board of directors toured the building and had nothing but compliments. We are happy in our new home."

Top: Dining and multi-purpose space.
Left: Servery.

152

Planning Design Research Corporation

1200 Smith
Suite 1100
Houston, TX 77002
713.739.9050
713.739.7246 (Fax)
www.pdrcorp.com
askpdr@pdrcorp.com

Planning Design Research Corporation

Planning Design Research Corporation

Schlumberger Limited Headquarters
Houston, Texas

The petroleum and natural gas industry needs no introduction to Schlumberger Limited, the world's leading oilfield services company. Founded in 1926 and active today in some 80 countries, the company wanted its new downtown Houston headquarters to represent a low-key portrayal of a global high-technology enterprise. Indeed, the new, two-floor, 46,000-square-foot facility for 102 employees, designed by Planning Design Research Corporation, facility, is the epitome of effectiveness and self-assurance. More importantly, its accommodations—including a ground floor

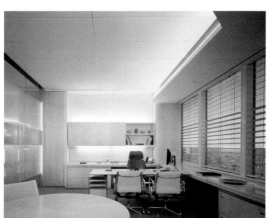

reception area, executive suite (reception, executive offices, boardroom, dining and commercial kitchen), private and open offices, internal stair and glass bridge, conference rooms, videoconference rooms, audit rooms, coffee bars and lunch room—jointly constitute an excellent working environment. Its layered spaces are structured as a visually transparent periphery of glazed private offices, circulation loop, and core areas finished in solid, opaque and reflective surfaces. Not only do they provide daylight for all employees, superior HVAC and lighting, and 10-foot ceilings, they sustain a safe, efficient and attractive environment. Their museum-quality art collection and sleek modern furnishings--including reupholstered Eames chairs and new, custom-designed furniture in sycamore and white lacquer--even comes with LEED-CI Silver certification. Schlumberger clearly belongs here as much as in the oil field.

Above: Conference room.
Above left: Stairs.
Left: Bridge.
Below left: Private office.
Opposite: Reception.
Photography: Jon Miller/ Hedrich Blessing.

Planning Design Research Corporation

International Energy Company
Houston, Texas

Businesses are discovering that even fixed assets—including real estate—can now respond quickly to a changing global economy. Just six months after an International Energy Company announced its relocation, a new, five-floor, 250,000-square-foot North American headquarters has been designed, documented and built for 800 employees in Houston. The facility, encompassing reception, executive offices, general office space and cafeteria, was designed by Planning Design Research Corporation to establish an "embassy-like" air of quality, dignity and function for the company. Developed like an upscale hotel or corporate conference center to house everyday activities and special events involving visiting dignitaries, the executive floor features gracious gathering rooms equipped for such specific functions as public announcements, private dinners, global video meetings and living room-style conversations. The award-winning, superbly crafted interiors exemplify classic modern style. Fitted out with ribbon mahogany, makore, wenge and other fine woods, leather, textiles, carpet, onyx, stainless steel, glass and a variety of lighting sources, they are highlighted by custom-made furniture pieces from noted designer Wayne Braun. Expressing his satisfaction with the results, the company's senior most executive declared that the design would indeed aid the company's ability to generate successful business opportunities.

Top right: Executive dining room.

Above middle left: Cafeteria servery.

Above middle right: Cafeteria dining room.

Above: Living room.

Left: Elevator lobby.

Opposite: Conference room.

Photography: Mark Scheyer.

Planning Design Research Corporation

ConocoPhillips Wellness Center
Houston, Texas

How much does ConocoPhillips, America's third-largest integrated energy company, value its employees? A lot, judging from the company's impressive new, three-floor, 110,000-square-foot Wellness Center, created for the 3,000 employees at its global headquarters campus in Houston. The Wellness Center, designed by Planning Design Research Corporation, operates an ambitious program through its cardio-fitness, weight conditioning, spinning, Pilates, aerobics and mediation studios, basketball-volleyball gymnasium, five-lane competition swimming pool, and men's and women's lockers and showers. To pull it off, the design team worked closely with the base building architect and other consultants to design the

building from the inside out, optimizing the site, sunlight and landscaping for all occupants. Consequently, the same high quality materials and details used for the building's other campus-wide accommodations, including the reception area, conference center, Garden Café and medical facility, appear in the Wellness Center. Along with eucalyptus and English sycamore veneers, Calcutta gold marble, stainless steel, granite, carpet tile, rubber and wood athletic flooring, porcelain and glass tile, wellness enthusiasts will find classic modern furnishings and sophisticated lighting fixtures. Like love at first sight, over half of the employees signed up for active use within the first week of enrollment.

Right: Lockers and showers.
Below right: Cardio studio.
Bottom left: Garden Café.
Bottom right: Swimming pool.
Opposite: Campus reception area with sculpture by El Anatsui.
Photography: Scott McDonald/ Hedrich Blessing.

Planning Design Research Corporation

Vitol
North American Headquarters
Houston, Texas

Above: Entry.
Top right: Conference room.
Left: Reception.
Photography: Mark Scheyer.

Most of the new, one-floor, 20,000-square-foot North American headquarters of Vitol in Houston, designed by Planning Design Research Corporation, houses the 100-desk trading floor. That suits the international energy, shipping and commodity trading company, whose businesses are headquartered in Rotterdam and Geneva. However, the award-winning facility makes the most of the remaining space to produce an inviting, cohesive and grand contemporary environment for the reception area, executive offices and kitchen that prepares breakfasts and lunches for employees. To capitalize on the 55th floor site atop a downtown office building, colors and finishes are light and bright, and the ceiling is raised from the standard nine feet to 10 feet. Furthermore, English sycamore walls are "edge-laced" with matching fretwork to dramatize the light and establish a layering of materials and finishes, and a private living room and small meeting room flank the reception area, entirely glazed to connect the interior space to daylight and outdoor views. Such materials as white marble infused terrazzo flooring, green wool carpet, Roman travertine, white Irish linen fabric wallcovering, and classic modern furniture complete the image, giving a critical link in Vitol's global trading network the unexpected and pleasing appearance of a prestigious residence.

Perkins+Will

330 N. Wabash Ave.
Suite 3600
Chicago, IL 60611
312.755.0770
312.755.0775 (Fax)
www.perkinswill.com

Perkins+Will

Perkins+Will

Bank of America
Corporate Center Pilot Project
Charlotte, North Carolina

Sometimes an office is more than an office. For Bank of America, one of the world's largest financial institutions, the Corporate Center Pilot Project is a prime example. The Pilot Project, a three-floor, 70,482-square-foot renovation at the Bank's corporate headquarters in Charlotte, designed by Perkins+Will, creates a modern workplace to support such core values as "doing the right thing" and "leadership." The space, including private offices, open offices, conference rooms, associates hub, copy and storage rooms, IDF room, file rooms, mail room, wellness room and

pantry, attains numerous goals: meeting LEED Gold CI criteria, promoting recruitment and retention, supporting high technology, accommodating multiple workstyles, maintaining flexibility, encouraging collaboration, and integrating the Bank brand. An innovative "chassis plan" establishes a foundation for the design. This interior infrastructure remains constant from floor to floor, providing an architectural framework for diverse programmatic and workstyle requirements, and alteration at increased speed and minimum cost. As a result, the infrastructure, which

features a zoned space plan, modularity among all products, systems and materials, limited hard construction, movable walls, branding and signage, and systems and freestanding furniture "kit of parts," powerfully reinforces the Bank's drive to become the world's most admired company.

Top right: Elevator lobby.
Right: Open Office
Below left: Associate's Hub Café.
Bottom right: Wayfinding Signage.
Opposite: Associates hub.
Photography: Steve Hall/ Hedrich Blessing.

Perkins+Will

U.S. Green Building Council
Headquarters
Washington, D.C.

The U.S. Green Building Council has proven that as creator and advocate of the Leadership in Energy and Environmental Design (LEED) Green Building Rating System, it walks the talk. Its new and appealing 25,000-square-foot Washington, D.C. headquarters provides a exceptionally functional, healthy and collaborative workplace. Everyone involved in the development, from the Council's project team and Perkins + Will, the facility's architect and interior designer, to the MEP engineer, lighting designer and general contractor, handled it as a full dress rehearsal for the future of the construction industry. Not only has the project earned its required LEED for Commercial Interiors Platinum rating, it has produced a high-performance space where 113 employees enjoy maximum access to daylight, good air quality, and a flexible environment. Why did the project succeed? Among the chief reasons: a tightly integrated building team; an open plan environment with private offices located away from the perimeter; 42-inch panels and low-height planters; multifunctional spaces designed for work and special events; materials with substantial recycled and renewable content; and efficient, resource-conserving MEP systems. Observes Rich Fedrizzi, the Council's CEO,

"We are already seeing an increase in collaboration and productivity as a result of the design scheme."

Top left: Reception area.
Top right: Conference room.
Left: Café.
Opposite: Open plan office.
Photography: Prakash Patel.

Perkins+Will

Haworth Showroom
Washington, D.C.

Right: Entry lobby.

Bottom right: Conference room.

Opposite: Manager's workstation with conference area.

Photography: Nick Merrick/ Hedrich Blessing.

Washingtonians who fondly remember the Hecht Company, once a leading department store chain, will be pleased to know its former flagship store is open for business again. The ambitious new Haworth Washington, D.C. showroom occupies a 20,000-square-foot space, designed by Perkins+Will, on the second floor of the historic structure, joining other tenants in a vital retail and entertainment district in downtown Washington. The showroom, which incorporates a sales office and conference facility, presents the Haworth brand platform of Adaptable Workspace, Designed Performance and Global Perspective in a dynamic setting of the company's office furniture products. By combining good design and engineering, for example, it demonstrates the benefits of environments that are both functional and beautiful. By showcasing the concept of "workspaces," it highlights the power of fully integrated interior architectural systems. By taking a holistic approach to product development, it forges a visible link between user satisfaction and productivity. Yet the design does more, giving visitors a unique view of sustainability from social, environmental and economic perspectives. Best of all, it illustrates how well Haworth products suit the design sensibilities of the design community and the economic concerns of corporate and institutional organizations in the nation's capital.

Perkins+Will

GameTap
Atlanta, Georgia

Perkins+Will's Interiors team was commissioned to design a space for the relocation and expansion of Turner Broadcasting's online game service, GameTap. The service has grown explosively since its debut in April 2005, and GameTap now offers more than 1,000 licensed games to its subscribers. Users from around the world visit GameTap's website and enjoy playing video titles from the vast library, including old favorites such as Pong and PacMan. Perkins+Will was charged with creating a space to accommodate collaboration among a group of highly creative programmers and management. The project includes a reception area, individual workspaces and offices, as well as inviting spaces to encourage collaboration among GameTap employees. The project is located in a warehouse redevelopment of 40,000 sq. ft. in downtown Atlanta. Care was taken to maximize natural daylight and overcome the lack of windows in the warehouse. The Perkins+Will Interiors team worked closely with the client, and the space reflects the essence of Turner Broadcasting and GameTap. Subtle design elements incorporate the Turner logo, while cleverly integrating graphics from different games into the workspaces. The result is a space that respects the brand and the building, while bringing warmth and human scale to the environment.

Top left: Lobby.
Top right: Reception area.
Above: Café.
Left: Corridor detail.
Photography: Nick Merrick/ Hedrich Blessing.

POLLACK architecture

111 Maiden Lane
Suite 350
San Francisco, CA 94108
415.788.4400
415.788.5309 (Fax)
www.pollackarch.com

POLLACK architecture

POLLACK architecture

Jansport
Corporate Headquarters
San Leandro, California

Jansport, a VF Corporation subsidiary noted for its backpacks, luggage and apparel, is back on the West Coast- where three young Seattle entrepreneurs founded it in 1967. The company recently relocated its headquarters from Appleton, Wisconsin to a new, one-floor, 22,000-square-foot facility, designed by San Francisco-based POLLACK architecture.

Located within an office park in San Leandro, California, the industrial-style private offices, teaming areas, showroom, warehouse and cafeteria use minimal resources in creative ways to honor Jansport's informal roots, supporting an aggressive expansion of product offerings and a re-energized corporate image. That the project took 10 weeks and was built

for $40 per square foot reflects the design team's creativity and responsiveness to Jansport. Numerous details feature inspired recycling, including sliding "barn doors" made from salvaged wood floorboards, polished existing concrete floors, open-joist ceilings and office construction. Yet the award-winning design also brings energy to the existing building, from the public

sequence which features a 100-foot-long space that highlights brand imagery and product displays, to dramatic showrooms framed by concrete walls and "barn doors," outfitted with white-lacquered display cases. The staff areas, which are simple and open, are flooded with daylight. Jansport observes that POLLACK architecture "exceeded our expectations."

Top left: Detail of showroom.
Top right: Reception area.
Above: Entrance to reception area and showroom.
Opposite bottom: Showroom.
Photography: César Rubio.

POLLACK architecture

Buchalter Nemer
Los Angeles, California

Even as law firms follow corporate clients worldwide, savvy attorneys are increasing operational flexibility and lowering construction costs in their offices. Consider the impressive new, four-floor, 75,000-square-foot Los Angeles headquarters office for Buchalter Nemer, designed by POLLACK architecture. A 160-attorney firm founded in 1948, Buchalter Nemer maintains additional offices in San Francisco, Orange County and Phoenix. Having retained POLLACK architecture to design the San Francisco and Irvine, California offices, it invited the architect to apply space standards, developed for earlier projects, to its downtown Los Angeles location. How was space reduced per attorney from 650 to 525 square feet, construction costs trimmed, or collaboration improved without compromising the finely detailed and finished contemporary environment Buchalter Nemer sought?

POLLACK split the budget into public, private and support areas, and developed appropriate details and finishes for each one. Thus, reception areas, private offices, work stations, library, training center, conference center, lounges, executive bar and lounge, catering area and lunchroom reflect specific degrees of visibility. The highly visible top floor, furnished with rich, earthy materials and furnishings houses the firm's extensive art collection. Virginia Banker, Buchalter Nemer's director of operations, declares "The design team understands how a law office must function."

Below left: Attorneys' lounge.
Below right: Reception area.
Opposite top left: Conference center.
Opposite top right: Breakout area and conference center.
Photography: César Rubio.

POLLACK architecture

POLLACK architecture Studios
San Francisco, California

When POLLACK architecture relocated 32 employees to Maiden Lane, in the heart of Union Square, it did what any sensible practitioner would do- it turned the design of its new, 8,300-square-foot studio into an opportunity to practice what it teaches clients. Having examined the root of the practice's passion, business drivers and culture, the design team developed a true designers' design studio: open, collaborative and exciting. It's not a simple solution, however. The space straddles three buildings, with floors varying over 36 inches in elevation. Fortunately, the dynamic design overcomes its constraints. Everything is visible from the front door. Transparent to the studio, the reception area and main conference room are housed in a partial glass pavilion hovering 30 inches above the rest of the space. The studio

itself, a wide, open expanse, fully exploits its north- and east-facing windows to flood the space with diffused natural light. The library and team work areas, situated at the heart of the design process, is a 36-foot-long work counter perfect for selecting finishes, holding informal meetings and hosting cocktail parties alike. Shouldn't everyone have a great workplace—like this?

Below: Studio.
Bottom left: Conference room.
Bottom right: Library.
Opposite: Reception area.
Photography: César Rubio.

POLLACK architecture

The Mechanics Bank
San Francisco, California

Ground-floor retail space offers an exceptional opportunity to communicate with the public as well as conduct business, and that's what The Mechanics Bank is doing with its new San Francisco flagship retail branch in the heart of the Financial District. The modern, one-level, 3,760-square-foot space (administrative functions occupy an upper floor) has been designed by POLLACK architecture as an expression of The Mechanics Bank brand, as well as a convenient banking location. What passersby see is a stately banking hall where a vaulted ceiling illuminated by stylish pendant fixtures presides over a large safe

deposit vault covered with shimmering glass tile, a sleek, custom-designed teller line finished in wood with marble counters, and a banking platform of timeless wood and leather furniture. It's an appropriate image for a bank with 33 retail and commercial banking offices and over $2.5 billion in assets, a local institution founded in 1905 and still owned and operated by the Downer family as one of the largest banks headquartered in the Bay Area. Equally important, the sidewalk view of a place where business owners can conduct business and personal banking has proved so compelling that the branch exceeded its annual projections within months after opening.

Top: Storefront view.
Above left: Teller line and banking platform.
Above right: Ceiling detail.
Photography: César Rubio.

Roger Ferris + Partners, LLC

285 Riverside Avenue
Westport, CT 06880
203.222.4848
203.222.4856 (Fax)
www.ferrisarch.com

Roger Ferris + Partners, LLC

Roger Ferris + Partners, LLC

Waterworks Inc.
Corporate Headquarters
Danbury, Connecticut

Left: Entry rotunda and tower.

Below: Private offices and open work area.

Bottom: Conference room and stair.

Opposite: Main corridor.

Photography: Paúl Rivera/arch-photo.com

Perhaps because it began as a plumbing supply business in 1923, Waterworks houses its headquarters in a complex of industrial buildings in Danbury, Connecticut, where office and warehouse coexist side by side. But the facility's no-frills industrial quality might startle customers of the specialty retailer of luxury bath products, whose exclusive bath fittings, fixtures and other goods represent the best that money can buy. Now, the headquarters has been upgraded with a new, two-story, 23,200-square-foot addition, designed by Roger Ferris + Partners. The addition creates a modern, open environment that unifies the existing buildings functionally and architecturally on a site constrained by wetlands to the east and west, a runway for Danbury Airport to the south, and Backus Road, a busy thoroughfare, to the north. While it reprises the brick "edge" projected by the complex along Backus Road, it exchanges an inconspicuous front door tucked into the east façade for a powerful entrance defined by a new, metal-clad rotunda and companion glass-and-aluminum tower. The expansive spirit continues inside, where an open "warehouse"-style setting of exposed structure and ceilings, aluminum and glass office fronts, and minimally detailed modern furnishings could be a suitable setting for Waterworks products.

Roger Ferris + Partners, LLC

Investment Firm
Greenwich, Connecticut

Not every architectural masterpiece gets a second life, considering how idiosyncratic shapes, unusual floorplates and unyielding structural systems can thwart prospective successors to original occupants. Happily, a new, one-floor, 31,000-square-foot office, designed by Roger Ferris + Partners for an investment firm which is a hedge fund manager, has made a modern, cost-effective and stimulating workplace from one such masterpiece, the former headquarters of American Can Company in Greenwich, Connecticut, originally designed by Skidmore Owings & Merrill. Visitors to the investment firm's private offices, open office areas, conference rooms, lounge, pantry and fitness area might not even notice the restrictions imposed by a building completed in 1970. How did the new scheme accommodate the original design's nearly overpowering ceiling of reinforced concrete beams? For Roger Ferris + Partners, the solution was to integrate the investment firm's detailed programming requirements, a custom-designed lighting scheme, and a modern architectural vocabulary of aluminum, glass, maple veneer millwork, carpet and limestone flooring with the existing building shell, working with the repetitive spacing of the ceiling rather than resisting it. The sensitivity of the design was not lost on the investment firm's personnel. Upon entering the office for the first time, one officer declared, "I feel energized by the architecture and lighting."

Roger Ferris + Partners, LLC

Roger Ferris + Partners, LLC
Westport, Connecticut

Distinguished for creating architecture, interior design, master planning, product design and graphic design that offer unique, contextual solutions to clients' needs, Roger Ferris + Partners, an architecture firm founded in 1986, recently faced an atypical yet familiar challenge: expanding its own office in Westport, Connecticut. Its new, two-story, 12,000-square-foot facility excels not only as a functional space, but also as a sensitive adaptation of the 19th-century tannery building along the Saugatuck River that houses it. Since the original brick-clad, wood column-and-beam structure and the glass enclosed addition constructed in the early 1980s on the east or riverside façade—separated by long corridors on both levels—are clearly the offspring of different times and techniques, the new environment exposes their differences to heighten the contrast and drama. The lower level features the architecture studio and studio conference room in the tannery portion, articulated in exposed brick walls and exposed wood structure, along with partners' offices and administrative functions in the addition, sheathed in glass walls and finished ceilings. On the upper level, which serves as the main

Top: Reception.

Above: Architecture studio.

Left: Private office.

Opposite: Corridor.

Photography: Paúl Rivera/arch-photo.com

Roger Ferris + Partners, LLC

reception area, the corridor is "pinched" to induce a forced perspective to the public conference room and dining area, using the "pinched" wall—one of many walls acting as a gallery for the firm's modern art collection—to enclose additional offices and the materials library. Careful detailing separates old from new throughout the office. Reveals keep new convection covers from touching existing brick walls along the west façade, for example, while changes in flooring materials mark the transition from studio to offices, and floating sheetrock ceiling planes bring modernity to corridors while discreetly concealing lighting and HVAC systems. Yet these aesthetic considerations have not overshadowed concern for the comfort of staff and visitors. Indoors, sandblasted original beams are juxtaposed against minimal white walls of sheetrock and painted brick to fill interiors with light even when they lack direct exposure to the building's sweeping views. On the roof, a new outdoor meeting space stands atop recycled rubber roof decking and reinforced structural support. If the facility makes visitors long for equally inviting accommodations, that's by design too.

Top left: Studio conference room.
Top right: Café/dining area.
Bottom left: Library.

RTKL Associates Inc.

1250 Connecticut Avenue
4th Floor
Washington, DC 20036
202.833.4400
202.887.5168 (Fax)
www.rtkl.com

RTKL Associates Inc.

Inter-American Development Bank Auditorium and Conference Center
Washington, D.C.

New construction usually comes in compact packages in Washington, D.C., where height restrictions and other planning constraints favor high-density development. Fortunately, such conditions don't preclude good design. Consider the Inter-American Development Bank's new, eight-floor, 35,000-square-foot auditorium and conference center, designed by RTKL Associates. For the Bank, established in 1959 to foster sustainable economic and social development in Latin America and the Caribbean, the search for space has taken it above and below grade. The transformation of a 55-foot-wide alley between its two existing headquarters buildings on New York Avenue into a centralized conferencing facility with a 500-seat auditorium, two 250-seat conference rooms and roof garden was complicated by the need for a street level

entrance for public functions, horizontal connections at upper levels for staff traveling between buildings, a vertical connection to an existing kitchen, and a five-floor height limit to preserve windows in offices on either side. The award-winning modern design places the conference rooms each on a separate upper level and the auditorium, which can convert from a flat-floor assembly function to a terraced performing arts function, 50 feet below grade—isolated from street noise yet opening a long-awaited "window into the IDB."

Top: Main entrance.
Above: Typical conference room.
Left: Exterior.
Opposite: Auditorium.
Photography: Erik Kvalsvik, Ron Blunt.

186

RTKL Associates Inc.

Consulting Client
Maryland

Anyone who insists the traditional office—comprising private offices along a building's perimeter and open workstations and other support functions in its interior space—is irrelevant should look harder. A consulting client recently asked RTKL Associates Inc. to design two facilities employing this time-honored scheme, along with conference rooms, laboratories, and pantries, at two Maryland locations, a one-floor, 20,000-square-foot space for 192 employees and a five-floor, 160,000-square-foot space for 1,097 employees. To maintain needed privacy and confidentiality without succumbing to an environment of dull and dark corridors, the design team focused on employing forms, materials and finishes that could distribute natural light.

Frosted glass and textured fabrics, for example, appear strategically in reception, conference rooms, building corners, and ends of corridors to transmit and diffuse daylight. By contrast, a variety of techniques mitigates the monolithic walls created by rows of offices: administrative work stations allowing unobstructed views of the exterior, canted and curved walls breaking up the orthogonal rigidity of corridors, and accent colors and angled ceiling features adding interest and acting as beacons for areas of shared use, such as conference rooms, printer areas and pantry. The benefit for employees and visitors: Clean, well-lighted and unexpectedly lively places.

Opposite: Reception.

Below middle: Conference center.

Bottom right: Open administrative area.

Bottom left: Touchdown workstations.

Bottom right: Typical corridor.

Photography: Anice Hoachlander.

RTKL Associates Inc.

General Motors
Government Relations Office
Washington, D.C.

Right: Office suite entry vestibule.

Far right: Conference center entry.

Bottom right: Breakout lobby for conference center.

Opposite bottom left: Administrative workstation.

Opposite bottom right: Lounge seating in conference center.

Photography: Erik Kvalsvik.

Like many other organizations maintaining offices in the nation's capital, the new, one-floor, 20,000-square-foot Government Relations Office for General Motors, designed by RTKL Associates, helps the company recognized as the world's largest automaker for 75 years to communicate with the federal government. It's a formidable task for a business that employs some 284,000 people, manufactures cars and trucks in 33 countries and sold 9.1 million vehicles in 2006. The award-winning facility actually shelters two operations with separate entrances: the office suite, with 24 private offices, five administrative workstations, conference rooms, and reception area, and the conference center, with conference rooms, reception area, and other public spaces. Each is "branded" as a GM facility with its own unique mission. The office suite, inspired by innovation, vehicles and the open road, uses dark carpet as a background for satin-finished wood, brushed stainless steel and frosted glass to help instill employee pride. In the conference center, highly polished stone, leather upholstered panels featuring a chromed GM logo, and display walls finished in glossy GM automotive paint express a showroom aesthetic to showcase GM's innovations and contributions to society. An appreciative GM characterizes the project as "beautifully designed and completed in record time."

RTKL Associates Inc.

Whiteford, Taylor & Preston, LLP
Baltimore, Maryland

Renovating in place has its pros and cons. On the plus side, it enables an organization to avoid moving. However, phased construction inevitably disrupts the routines of individuals and groups by sending them in and out of "swing" spaces as their offices are rebuilt. Judging from the recent remodeling of the four-floor, 89,000-square-foot office of Whiteford, Taylor & Preston, a Baltimore-based law firm founded in 1933 that has over 155 attorneys, the outcome amply compensates for the inconvenience. RTKL Associates' transformation of the workspace, where a traditional arrangement of private window offices and interior secretarial stations and support areas has been reorganized and updated, introduces a modern conference center on the 19th floor, complete with conference rooms, law

library, visiting attorneys area, and attorney lounge. Though the design quietly reinforces the image of the firm, which serves major national companies and local businesses, the introduction of wood throughout the practice floors—particularly for secretarial stations—as well as the conference center, the selection of handsome, transitional furnishings, and the installation of sophisticated lighting have instilled a look of timeless quality in the workplace. Greatly pleased with the makeover, Whiteford, Taylor & Preston has retained RTKL Associates for additional work.

Top left: Conference center. staircase.

Top middle: Curved wall.

Top right: Vestibule of conference center.

Right: Attorney lounge.

Photography: Erik Kvalsvik.

Sasaki Associates Inc.

64 Pleasant Street
Watertown, MA 02472
617.926.3300
617.924.2748 (Fax)
www.sasaki.com

77 Geary Street
4th Floor
San Francisco, CA 94108
415.776.7272
415.202.7403 (Fax)

Sasaki Associates Inc.

Sasaki Associates Inc.

Monitor Group
San Francisco, California

Top left: Reception area.

Top right: Kitchen area in community space.

Above: Community space.

Left: Team Room.

Opposite: Community space corridor.

Photography: Robert Benson.

The business world's growing preference for open workplaces hasn't deterred organizations from flourishing in private offices. Consider the impressive new, single-floor, 28,000-square-foot San Francisco office of Monitor Group, designed by Sasaki Associates. It's considerably more than an aggregation of private offices. Monitor Group, a Cambridge, Massachusetts-based global strategy and management consulting firm, developed it to combine Global Business Network, a Bay Area company it acquired, with its own San Francisco office. To help some 100 employees to work at maximum potential, the design had to express Monitor Group's global brand without suppressing local identities, encourage collaboration among colleagues through opportunities for social learning and teamwork, and instill a sense of place throughout the anonymous, block-long floor plate. The space has won praise since opening day. Its grid of "cross streets," intersected by a diagonal "main street" terminating at two elliptical community spaces, abounds in daylight and outdoor views, aided by full glazing of perimeter offices, natural finishes, bright accent colors, handsome modern furnishings, and community spaces that invite casual use with lounge seating, resource libraries, and food service. Jon Proffitt, Monitor Group's director of real estate, recently declared, "I am very proud to have been part of this team."

Sasaki Associates Inc.

Hershey Entertainment & Resorts
Hershey, Pennsylvania

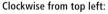

While life is sweet for Hershey Entertainment & Resorts, owner and operator of such entertainment destinations as Hershey Park in Hershey, Pennsylvania, home of The Hershey Company and its chocolate confections, it recently became even more so. Thanks to a new 75,000-square-foot headquarters, designed by Sasaki Associates for two of three floors in downtown's historic (1915) Hershey Press Building, all 150 headquarters employees share the same space for the first time. In addition, they enjoy a striking workplace that combines respect for the past with a forward-looking workplace that celebrates the entertainment company and embraces sustainable design. The new executive offices, general offices, boardroom, reception, executive dining, call center, and gallery space clearly transcend a conventional relocation. With its own future linked to that of its hometown, HE&R regularly develops new construction and preserves existing commercial structures to benefit residents and tourists alike. The rebirth of the Hershey Press Building, which began with a restoration of its brick industrial shell, incorporates such original elements as the columns, floor slabs and ornamental stair, and introduces a contemporary, white interior appointed in Pennsylvania bluestone, cherry millwork, maple plank flooring and transitional furnishings, where the freestanding boardroom's cherry wood-clad "box" resembles an elegant package of bonbons.

Clockwise from top left: Boardroom, reception area, executive dining, call center, CEO conference room.

Opposite: "The Walk" gallery space.

Photography: Robert Benson.

Sasaki Associates Inc.

Sullivan & Worcester, LLP
Boston, Massachusetts

A 200-attorney law firm that prides itself on handling major corporate work worldwide while retaining a small firm's collegiality, Sullivan & Worcester maintains offices in Boston, New York and Washington, D.C., as well as international alliances in Europe, Asia and the Middle East. The firm recently developed what is now indispensable for many law offices: a state-of-the-art conference center and reception in the Boston office's 21st floor, designed by Sasaki Associates as part of a five-floor, 105,840-square-foot remodeling of existing facilities for 270 employees. The conference center simultaneously exploits spectacular views of Boston's harbor and skyline and encloses conference rooms with floor-to-ceiling, sandblasted glass interior walls to let daylight reach interior spaces while preserving privacy. Its new environment gives Sullivan & Worcester a fresh, International Style look, complete with new furniture and finish standards, that is as comfortable as it is attractive. Nine conference rooms seating six to 24 people discreetly integrate screens, projectors and other AV/IT equipment and a mobile wall partition into a setting of plush wool carpet, drapery sheers lining the window wall, and credenzas in birdseye maple with stone tops cantilevered from silk fabric wrapped walls between rooms, blending tradition and modernity as the firm does.

Top left: Reception area.

Top right: Conference center reception seen from elevator lobby.

Right: Elevator lobby.

Opposite bottom left: Typical conference room.

Opposite bottom right: Breakout area along conferencing suite.

Photography: Richard Mandelkorn.

Sasaki Associates Inc.

BTU Ventures, Inc.
Waltham, Massachusetts

Many businesses might hesitate to simultaneously retain an existing build-out, saving time and money, and project an image of relaxed elegance. Nevertheless, that's the successful story of the new, one-floor, 10,000-square-foot headquarters of BTU Ventures, in Waltham, Massachusetts, designed by Sasaki Associates. BTU Ventures is the venture capital arm of the BTU Group, a private equity group that focuses on the midstream and downstream segments of the energy value chain in emerging markets. Its new facility is particularly satisfying for its 40 employees because the space, comprising a lobby, library/reception, offices, CEO office, boardroom, kitchen/lunch room and confer-ence/training room, resolves a potentially awkward space resulting from the skylights of the tenant below while dramatically upgrading exist-ing construction standards. Among the project's innova-tions are the new, curving wood wall that directs circulation and doubles as an art gallery, the library/recep-tion and CEO office, both positioned to maximize water views, movable art panels for concealing base building doors, frosted pivot doors and sliding panels designed so the training room and kitchen/lunch room can open to each other and the office space, and the contemporary furnishings, cherry wood trim, and neutral paint, carpet and upholstery that make the facility both stylish and comfortable.

Top left: Art gallery.
Top right: Conference/training room.
Left: CEO office.
Bottom left: Library/reception.
Photography: Robert Benson.

SKB Architecture and Design

1818 N Street, NW
Suite 510
Washington, DC 20036
202.332.2434
202.328.4547 (Fax)
www.skbarch.com

SKB Architecture and Design

SKB Architecture and Design

Jenner & Block LLP
New York, New York

Bright, airy and modern are not typical law office attributes, but they describe the new, single-floor, 32,000-square-foot New York office of Jenner & Block, designed by SKB Architecture & Design. A Chicago-based firm, founded in 1914 and respected for work in corporate transactions and major litigation, Jenner & Block wanted the facility to reflect a culture combining respect for the law with the highest legal standards and a collegial atmosphere. The outcome, serving 70 attorneys and support personnel, achieves these goals by uniquely blending traditional and contemporary concepts. Private offices and conference rooms line the perimeter as usual, while work stations, mini-conferencing center, main conference room with attached catering station, library, file room, lunchroom, lobby and reception occupy the interior. However, the interior also acknowledges a 37th floor location and the firm's desire for a fresh, timely image. Vertical and horizontal planes extend the perceived space, with clear glass doors at corner offices and conference rooms, orange glass partitions dividing work stations, macassar ebony wood paneling complementing amber walls, and travertine and marble enriching the reception and lobby areas. Completed with contemporary furnishings, the "Danish design meets Bauhaus" environment gives Jenner & Block impressive credentials in New York.

Above: Reception seating.

Top right: Entry to reception.

Right: View of corridor from reception.

Opposite bottom left: Large conference room.

Opposite bottom right: Small glass conference room.

Photography: Paul Warchol.

SKB Architecture and Design   Miller & Chevalier
Washington, DC

Sometimes the best location for an organization needing new space is its existing premises. For Miller & Chevalier, a prestigious, Washington, D.C. law firm founded in 1920, this strategy has produced outstanding results. The recently finished, two-and-a-half-floor, 120,000-square-foot renovation, designed by SKB Architecture & Design, keeps 240 employees in a downtown building that is conveniently located, offers views of the White House and the Mall, and features a 12-story, naturally lighted atrium. Of course, to improve attorney office counts and overall operations as part

of a 15-year growth plan, SKB Architecture & Design has implemented numerous critical changes, such as increasing the efficiency of square footage per attorney, creating a mid-floor reception area and centralized conferencing center, adding a multi-purpose, dividable meeting room, developing a litigation and records center, reducing the size of the library and centralizing its location, and redesigning secretarial work stations and attorney filing to improve work flow. This pragmatic transformation boasts dramatic flourishes, nevertheless. Within the two-story spaces

inserted in the new, centralized reception and conferencing center, a signature, two-story, articulated wall that doubles as sculpture clearly has the power of art to impress people.

Top left: Conferencing center.
Top right: Interior atrium.
Above right: Entry from elevator lobby.
Right: Breakout area of conferencing center.
Below right: Workstation detail.
Opposite: Interior atrium seating.
Photography: Ron Solomon.

SKB Architecture and Design

PG&E Corporation
Washington, D.C.

Left: Suite entry.
Above: Reception seating.
Directly below left: Main conference room.
Below left: Workroom/lounge.
Bottom left: Typical office.
Photography: Ron Solomon.

The mandate for this major California energy company's government affairs Washington, DC office was to exemplify its corporate philosophy by the use of energy efficient lighting components, minimize electrical consumption and use green/sustainable materials throughout the design. In support of the corporate mission, lighting power loads are lower than the progressive California 2005 Title 24 energy-efficiency standard by 10% and meet the Office Lighting Standard requirements. This project is a beta testing site for an integrated lamping system whose output adjusts automatically in response to available daylight. Floor to ceiling glass along the perimeter office corridor wall extends natural day lighting into internal areas. Bamboo flooring was used both as a reception entry statement and as a directional element through the gallery into the main conference room. Sealed exposed concrete columns in the reception area and main conference room punctuate the space and allow the occupant to relate directly to the base building structure.

SKB Architecture and Design

Crowell & Moring LLP
New York, New York

Fifty-three attorneys left a major law firm in 1979 to start Crowell & Moring, and their "tough yet approachable," community-minded and pragmatic practice was much in evidence recently when the nearly 350-attorney firm opened its first New York office with 70 employees in a newly remodeled, one-floor, 30,000-square-foot space, designed by SKB Architecture & Design. The facility was developed on a tight schedule and set budget to let the firm take a short-term lease in premises vacated by a corporation. Under these circumstances, the design team focused on "branding" the reception area with new client conference rooms to help establish the firm's identity in New York, while retaining existing private window offices to house partners and associates, and reconfiguring existing interior workstations to accommodate secretaries and paralegals. Such materials as maple flooring and panels, silk acoustical panels, carpet, solid walnut accent planks, clear and colored glass and sophisticated lighting are combined to produce a contemporary architectural environment where the attorneys can interact with clients, communicating the message that this international law firm is now a major player in town.

Above left: Reception desk detail.

Above right: Reception seating.

Left: Conference room.

Below left: View of reception from entry.

Photography: Paul Warchol.

207

SKB Architecture and Design

The World Bank Country Office
Dhaka, Bangladesh

Sharing a site northwest of central Dhaka, Bangladesh near Louis Kahn's National Assembly with the Asian Development Bank, The World Bank Country Office occupies a new, five-story, 80,000-square-foot building, designed by SKB Architecture & Design, that adroitly combines minimal use of land with maximum use of renewable resources. Little is wasted providing private offices, work stations, conference rooms, lunchroom and fitness center for 136 people. Not only are over 60 indigenous trees planted on site, there are a grass roof, on-site wastewater treatment, carpet incorporating recycled nylon fiber, thermal break curtainwall with heat absorbing insulated glass, operable windows, and computer-

managed air conditioning. Even the all-white interiors use daylight almost exclusively during working hours. For all the functionality, the structure has its symbolism. To accommodate program requirements, vehicular access, a potential connection to the Asian Development Bank, and natural light for all occupants, the building consists of two sections. The first, reprising Dhaka's contemporary architecture of concrete frame and masonry infill, aligns with the city's new, orthogonal grid and the Quibla (towards Mecca). Paradoxically, the second is a modernist glass structure with an engineered sunshade (brise soleil) to cut heat gain, aligned with the solar path much as old Dhaka is.

Top left: Atrium.
Top right: Reception.
Left: Lunchroom with garden view.
Bottom left: Terracotta wall.
Photography: Mark Baughman, AIA, IIDA.

Staffelbach Design Associates Inc.

2525 Carlisle
Dallas, TX 75201
214.452.1283
214.224.3075 (Fax)
www.staffelbach.com

Staffelbach Design Associates Inc.

2100 Ross Avenue
Dallas, Texas

"Take me to 2100 Ross Avenue." It's a request taxi and limousine drivers are hearing more and more in Dallas. Erected in 1982 as 2121 San Jacinto Street, the San Jacinto Center, a 33-story, 845,000-square-foot office building at the northernmost tip of the city's central business district, 2100 Ross Avenue is a powerful demonstration of how design can change the outlook for an existing property. When its new owners, IPC US REIT, a Canadian real estate investment trust that owns and manages principally Class A office buildings in mid- to large-sized U.S. cities and strong suburban markets, and the PNL Companies, a Dallas-based family of real estate investment entities active throughout the United States and Canada, retained Staffelbach Design Associates to direct a renovation, they launched a $3.5 million project that has altered more than just the lobby and streetscape. By studying the pedestrian traffic in the area and proposing to re-orient the entrance from San Jacinto Street, on the building's south side, to Ross Avenue, on the north side, Staffelbach enabled the distinctive, tripartite tower to accommodate an impressive entry plaza and soaring main lobby. Equally important, the design team's proposal created a direct connection for tenants of 2100 Ross Avenue to the Dallas Arts District, a vibrant and prestigious neighborhood at the new front door that is home to such established and emerging institutions as the Dallas Museum of Art, Nasher Sculpture Center, Morton H. Meyerson Symphony Center, Crow Collection of Asian Art, and the Dallas Center for the Performing Arts, whose opening in 2008 will introduce the Winspear Opera House, City Performance Hall, Grand Plaza, Annette Strauss Artist Square and Wyly Theater. Of course, significant changes were made to the existing structure in the course of the project, such as the removal of one of four granite-clad mechanical towers near the new entrance to visually

Top: Canopy framing view of main lobby.

Above: View of Ross Avenue and Guadalupe Cathedral from main lobby.

Opposite: Main lobby.

First overleaf: Entrance, canopy, pylons and trellis along Ross Avenue.

Second overleaf: Seating in main lobby.

Photography: Craig Kuhner.
Structural: Jaster-Quintanilla Dallas, LLP.
Architecture: GSR Andrade
Landscape: MESA

Staffelbach Design Associates Inc.

open the approach to the lobby, and the installation of a new canopy, pylons and trellis on the sidewalk to mark the new entrance and provide a transition between the monumental exterior scale and the human scale of the main lobby. Otherwise, the new and renovated interior spaces, including a conference center, elevator lobbies, garage elevators and management office as well as major lobbies, complete the makeover with glass and lighter finishes in wood and stone, timeless, classical furnishings, and a lighting scheme by Lang Lighting Design. A brighter, more expansive interior has emerged now that the three remaining mechanical towers have shed their dark granite for reflective glass, and some of the deep red marble flooring has yielded to natural granite. In a gesture towards its new neighbors, 2100 Ross Avenue even features a towering, 30-foot-high customized art wall as the focal point of the main lobby. The work of artist Paul Deeb and his firm, Vox Environmental Design, the frosted glass slab projects a dynamic light show on its skin to interact with people and architecture, turning each working day at 2100 Ross Avenue into a living work of performance art.

Tanager Design Group, Inc.
+
Mekus Studios, Ltd.
+
Jones Lang LaSalle

401 East Illinois Street
Suite 400
Chicago, IL 60611
312.644.3080
312.644.3086 (Fax)
www.tanagerdesigngroup.com

Tanager Design Group, Inc. + Mekus Studios, Ltd.

Motorola
mobilezone.chicago
Chicago, Illinois

Can Motorola walk the talk? A global leader in telecommunications equipment for broadband, embedded systems and wireless networks that describes itself as "powered by, driving, seamless mobility," Motorola recently departed from its suburban Chicago roots to open a showcase for mobility at a downtown Chicago location on North Michigan Avenue's fabled "Magnificent Mile." Indeed, the company's new, one floor, 35,000 square-foot mobilezone.chicago, designed by Tanager Design Group, Inc. in collaboration with Mekus Studios Ltd and project management by Jones Lang LaSalle, houses over 200 mobile employees and two employees stationed there daily; namely a concierge and a security agent, in a state-of-the-art "touchdown" work site. The "employee mobility center," which includes concierge entrance and visitor collaboration area, mobile offices, touchdown workstations, conference rooms, team rooms/focus rooms, corridors and a café, has been planned to incorporate Motorola's culture and experience in a three-dimensional space reflecting the traits of the "Moto" brand, encouraging innovation and challenging the status quo. To turn such high expectations into a practical working environment, Tanager developed a new prototype office that employs a carefully structured floor plan where curving walls play off straight ones, along with sophisticated direct and indirect lighting, modern, light and flexible furnishings, and Motorola's signature colors and graphics, to give multiple non-assigned workplaces a genuine sense of place. Tanager's close coordination with the Jones Lang LaSalle real estate team and Motorola — one of five design competitions won last year from the company — is revealed in the seamless environment

Above left: Mobility office.

Above middle: Focus room/ team room.

Above: Concierge entrance.

Opposite: Mobility center with workstations.

Photography: Jeff Millies/ Hedrich Blessing.

Tanager Design Group, Inc. + Mekus Studios, Ltd.

at the facility, starting when an employee arrives at the concierge entrance. Modeled to resemble a streamlined airport check-in, the entrance enables each mobile worker to register for work quickly and easily on a flat screen monitor and receive electronic security. Likewise, formal and informal meeting spaces promote flexibility and collaboration through multiple sizes, demountable walls and mobile furniture, so that team rooms and focus rooms can host gatherings as small as two people and as large as 50. The conferencing center comfortably accommodates 22 people with gallery seating for another 25. Walk the talk? Motorola has found that the design results in productive employees and a 38 percent increase in per person capacity over the traditional office layout, and is rolling out the concept in other locations around the world.

Right: Mobility workstations.

Below: Corridor.

Below middle right: Focus room/team room.

Bottom right: Café.

221

Tanager Design Group, Inc.

Motorola
SH1
Schaumburg, Illinois

First appearances count, and Motorola's recent design competition to remodel the entry to a complex of buildings at its headquarters in Schaumburg, Illinois—a critical example of a first appearance that suffered from a lack of clarity or connectivity to other facilities—acknowledges as much. Interestingly, when Tanager Design Group, Inc. won the assignment to design the entry, the scope of the project was redefined to include the entire first floor and reception at Sector Headquarters-1st Floor or SH1. The one-floor, 45,000-square-foot SH1 space is the central hospitality area for the complex and includes a lobby/reception, mobility center, conference rooms, multiple "touchdown" areas, wellness center and Starbucks Café, a facility that can accommodate over 500 people at one time. To improve wayfinding so that people can find their directions and reach their destinations, the design transforms the first floor into a series of visual cues to initiate a sense of horizontal and vertical flow. Through identification, repositioning, design, graphics and Motorola signature branding, people easily recognize enough elements of the "Moto" culture of seam-

Top left: Reception.

Top right: Focus room.

Above right: Mobility entrance.

Right: Wellness center entrance.

Opposite: Mobility area lounge seating.

Photography: Christopher M. Mekus, AIA/Mekus Studios Ltd. entrance.

Tanager Design Group, Inc.

less connectivity to guide themselves to the elevator lobby and upper floors of the seven-story entry building or to other destinations in the complex. Sector Headquarters 1 is both a vivid reminder that first appearances count—even for a global leader in telecommunications equipment for broadband, embedded systems and wireless networks—and good design can produce great first appearances and a flexible functional space.

Left: Mobility area.
Above: Conference room.
Bottom: Collaboration room/conference room.

Ted Moudis Associates

79 Madison Avenue
New York, NY 10016
212.308.4000
212.561.2020 (Fax)
www.tedmoudis.com

One Financial Place
440 South LaSalle Street
Chicago, IL 60605
312.663.0130
312.663.0138 (Fax)

Ted Moudis Associates

Ted Moudis Associates

America Online
New York, New York

For all the media frenzy about internet upstarts, America Online continues to thrive as the nation's second largest Web network, third largest online advertising network, and leading instant network, attracting 111 million unique visitors a month. Popular brands include AOL.com, Mapquest, AIM, Moviefone, ICQ, and Netscape. To keep the 1,200 plus employees in New York equally connected, productive and satisfied, the company recently developed a sleek, six-floor, 135,000-square foot office, designed by Ted Moudis Associates, celebrating openness and community. The design team developed a concept that establishes a central communal space interconnected by a simple staircase on each floor. Throughout the space there

is emphasis on transparency, accessibility and lighting, which subtly compensates wherever daylight is lacking. The minimalist vocabulary of full height glass office fronts, exposed ceilings and a color scheme of stark white with blue and yellow accents impart a palpable energy to the space. The main floor which houses the training rooms, video conferencing suite, hotelling clusters, boardroom and bistro is brought together through the use of a backlit neon ribbon of light. This clever yet simple detail of continuity, is evident and in its most pure form in this communal space. In fact, it's as fresh and inviting as AOL itself.

Top left: Interconnecting stair.

Top right: Breakout space at bistro and training area.

Above: Conference room.

Right: Reception area.

Opposite top left: Elevator lobby.

Opposite top right: Curving feature wall.

Photography: Peter Paige Photography.

Ted Moudis Associates

Ted Moudis Associates
New York, New York

Right: Open studio.

Bottom left: Library.

Bottom middle: Café.

Bottom right: Interconnecting stair.

Opposite: Reception area.

Opposite bottom left: Multi-purpose room.

Opposite bottom right: Presentation room.

Photography: Paul Warchol.

If a corporate design firm's office serves as a three-dimensional prospectus for itself, Ted Moudis Associates has created a blue chip asset in midtown Manhattan. The firm, which serves leading businesses and institutions nationally as well as internationally, has designed a stunning new 35,000-square-foot office split over two floors. Currently holding 115 employees it doubles as a workplace and a showroom. On entering the space visitors find themselves in a contemporary setting, one where sophisticated and streamlined details are abundant. The award winning space comprises of a reception area, open studio, administrative offices, resource library and multiple meeting facilities such as a presentation room, multi-purpose training rooms, breakout café and various open teaming spaces, all of which reflect the many facets of today's business environment. This is a setting where form and function truly are intertwined and visitors are invariably exposed to this as they travel through the space. The majority of the office is open plan and balances high density with good circulation. Furniture is held off from the windows to minimize dead ends and maximize the opportunities for staff to appreciate the views from the perimeter windows and increase exposure to direct sunlight. Private offices are restricted to a short length of perimeter wall on the 1st floor and a one size fits all policy for the workstations enables maximum flexibility for team growth and company wide expansion. Materials, furnishings and lighting are not only practical; they are unmistakably appealing for their lean profiles and minimal details. The fact that visitors express the desire to work here suggests Ted Moudis Associates knows its business and clients well.

Ted Moudis Associates

Khronos, LLC
New York, New York

What's an effective way to house a group of energetic and ambitious hedge fund managers in midtown Manhattan? At Khronos, the solution is a one-floor, 15,750-square foot office, designed by Ted Moudis Associates. This neatly tailored, modern space expresses the fast-moving, collaborative and demanding environment that today's financial markets seem to lean towards – without denying the need for moments of concentration, seclusion and relaxation. It's particularly effective in exploiting its L-shaped building. To make the floor plate efficient, the design establishes a natural flow of circulation from the entryway and conferencing suite into the main office space. The café is placed at the tip of the plan encouraging staff to take a few moments from their busy schedules for a little relaxation. The narrow "leg" of the L shape provides a natural location for HR, administration and IT, flowing effortlessly into the rest of the space, which accommodates the investment and accounting groups as well as multiple meeting rooms and the library. Every detail has its purpose. The private offices are enclosed by full height frameless glass walls to promote interaction and let natural light flow into the interior space. The only puncture to this transparent boundary is the introduction of a powerful Zebrano wood door detail that anchors the frontages. Relatively low ceiling heights are successfully articulated using multiple planes of acoustic tile, sheetrock and mirrored chrome that are married together by simple reveals. Furnishings complete the interior with clean, modern profiles and residential-style comfort. This attention to detail combined with the clever and articulated architectural solutions have equipped Khronos with the tools to manage their financial world.

Top left: Elevator lobby.
Top right: Waiting area.
Middle left: Conference room.
Middle right: Typical office front.

Above: Café.
Opposite: Reception.
Photography: Frank Ooms.

Ted Moudis Associates

Société Générale
Jersey City, New Jersey

Right: Café.

Below left: Café.

Below middle left: Private offices and open office area.

Bottom left: Interconnecting stair.

Photography: Peter Paige Photography.

Jersey City is visible just across the Hudson River from Manhattan, but relocating approximately 600 members of the operational staff at Societe Generale, a leading European financial services organization, from New York to New Jersey required a cultural change as well as a change of address. To alter the way employees use office space and expand the provisions available to them, Societe Generale developed a new, three-floor, 135,000-square foot "progressive office," designed by Ted Moudis Associates. One hallmark of the new spatial order was to re-evaluate the location of the private offices, the result being a one size fits all template that allows the open office staff to appreciate the surrounding window views and the abundance of natural daylight. Low partitions were also used in the furniture layouts allowing a clear vista within the large floor plates. The private offices incorporate full height glass fronts with sliding doors that minimize the impact on the already small footprint and allow all the staff to appreciate the amazing New York City views. Another significant change is the establishment of an extensive, multi-functional café to act as an energetic hub, providing interactive plasma displays as well as a "touchdown bar" and mixed seating styles to compensate for the vibrant city life left behind. Together with conference rooms, training rooms, interconnecting stair, and an elevator lobby where a "virtual receptionist" enables visitors to find contacts via an interactive console and telephone, these spaces manage to be cost-effective yet appealing — with spectacular views of lower Manhattan as a bonus.

TPG Architecture, LLP

360 Park Avenue South
New York, NY 10010
212.768.0800
212.768.1597 (Fax)

www.tpgarchitecture.com

TPG Architecture, LLP

TPG Architecture, LLP

Mansueto Ventures
New York, New York

All the ambivalence New Yorkers have felt towards the site of the World Trade Center in lower Manhattan since 2001 vanishes when the elevator doors open on the 29th floor of 7 World Trade Center, the new headquarters of Mansueto Ventures. This one-floor, 40,000-square-foot office for 190 employees of the publisher of *Inc.* and *Fast Company* magazines, designed by TPG Architecture, offers a boldly modern, elegantly Spartan, and emphatically collaborative way of working that could become a model for future workplaces. It's also one of the first tenant spaces in the first new building erected at ground zero. The symbolism isn't lost on Mansueto Ventures, a business established by Joe Mansueto, the founder and principal owner of Morningstar Inc. Once the company acquired the two magazines from Gruner + Jahr USA, it began looking for a new home not far from its existing midtown location. "When our general manager suggested we consider lower

Manhattan, I thought: 'Why not? We're entrepreneurial, just like our readers,'" recalls John Koten, CEO of Mansueto Ventures. Sending a confident message to its 1.44 million subscribers, the publisher has created an open, cooperative and forward-looking environment at 7 World Trade Center, a graceful glass skyscraper

Below left: Café.
Right: Elevator lobby.
Below right: Boardroom.
Bottom right: Reception.
Photography: Mikiko Kikuyama.

TPG Architecture, LLP

designed by Skidmore, Owings & Merrill. Mansueto's remarkable facility, comprising a reception area, private offices, open workstations, café, canteen, boardroom and various other meeting spaces, copy rooms, lockers and other support spaces, has been structured by TPG Architecture to promote collaboration among employees at all levels. It also exploits the stunning panorama of New York visible from the floor-to-ceiling windows enclosing the column-free interior. How unconventional the solution is can be sensed immediately at the entrance, which leads directly to the café, marked by a circular carpet set on the polished concrete floor, and a sweeping view of New York's harbor. Employees work here when they're not consuming bagged breakfasts and lunches, and the space summarizes the scheme of the entire facility with its blend of stylish yet functional contemporary furnishings, great views, and no-nonsense interior of bare floors (save for work stations) and exposed ceilings (except in enclosed areas) covered only by sound-absorbent fireproofing. Everything focuses on function, from

Top: Media wall.

Right: Breakout room.

Opposite: Open workstations.

Overleaf: Open workstations and private offices.

TPG Architecture, LLP

the small, identically-sized private offices along the periphery, enclosed in glass and sliding glass doors to admit daylight and views into the interior, to the small open workstations with low partitions, clustered into "turrets," "benches," and "pinwheels," and the core area, where interns perch on high stools at counters, copy rooms encourage employees to mingle, and lockers hold personal possessions workstations won't accommodate. There's a buzz of conversation among the open workstations, evoking the traditional newsroom. But a look here and there tells you this is not business as usual. A media wall for each magazine, for example, depicts the current issue's real-time page make-up on a grid of monitors. Corner spaces hold meetings rather than managers. And the traditional clutter inundating journalists' desks is nowhere to be seen, since almost all transactions are conducted electronically. The sleek workstations, made by Italy's Unifor, bested two leading American competitors because their versatility is matched by their simplicity. Of course, a great purging of desks and files preceded the move. "The housecleaning was good preparation for the new office," Koten jokes. Workers of the global economy, take note.

Right: Core area storage.

Bottom: Café serving counter and reception desk.

TVS Interiors

2700 Promenade Two   Atlanta
1230 Peachtree Steet NE   Chicago
Atlanta, GA 30309   Dubai
404.888.6600   Shanghai
404.888.6700 (Fax)
www.tvsinteriors.com

TVS Interiors

Country Music Television
Nashville, Tennessee

Launched in 1983, Country Music Television knows practically everything about country music, reaching some 83 million households annually. Since being purchased by MTV, the Nashville-based company experienced rapid growth and embarked upon a renovation of their 30,000 square-foot office space. Working with TVS Interiors, the company set upon an expansion from two to three floors. They knew they needed flexibility for future changes and a facility to house a lobby, open offices, private offices, conference rooms, break rooms, broadcast room, control room, announcer room and multi-function space. TVS Interiors' zoning plan helped CMT increase effectiveness and enhance collaboration. The former departmentalized setting with private offices lining the perimeter yielded to a more open office scheme featuring common workspace for

most employees. The private offices and service hallways are now located in the core while a popular circulation path borders the windows. Appointed in rustic finishes and colors reflecting the television unit's branding program, plus comfortable modern furnishings and numerous plasma screens,

the interiors gives CMT room to work and play.

Below: Radio booth.

Below middle left: Private office.

Below middle right: Lobby.

Bottom left: Open workstation.

Bottom right: Lounge beside radio booth and control room.

Opposite: Lobby and conference room.

Photography: Brian Gassel/ TVS Interiors

TVS Interiors

Investment Management Firm
Atlanta, Georgia

How does a design firm transform a long, narrow volume of bowling-alley-like space into an elegant office for an investment management firm? TVS Interiors transformed this 6,000 square-foot space into a classic modern design using rich materials, timeless furnishings and fine art. Applying corporate standards to the space and utilizing planning efficiencies, TVS Interiors brought daylight from the building's perimeter into the interior and added architectural variety. The space features such critical details as walls with custom millwork, breaking up the long axis of space and defining specific neighborhoods of activity. Clerestories and sliding glass doors for private offices let daylight filter into the interior. Materials such as sycamore and African mahogany wood, glass, aluminum and broadloom carpet contribute to the modern and sleek contemporary feel throughout the reception area, private offices, visitor's office, conference room, break room, open workspace and file/work room. In addition, a color palette of light neutral colors with clear contrasts and sophisticated direct and indirect lighting bring a classic Cinderella story of transformation by design to a happy ending.

Top left: Conference room.
Top right: Conference break out space.
Right: Enclosed office.
Opposite bottom middle: Breakout space.
Opposite bottom left: Open office and circulation.
Photography: Brian Gassel/ TVS Interiors.

245

TVS Interiors

Kimball Office
Chicago Showroom
Chicago, Illinois

A convenient location is seldom enough to attract the design community to an interior furnishings showroom in Chicago's River North neighborhood, where retail and to-the-trade businesses flourish. Kimball Showroom, a leading contract office furniture maker, has successfully developed a new, two-level, 9,900 square-foot showroom. Designed by TVS Interiors, the showroom is drawing designers to a location directly facing the Merchandise Mart. TVS Interiors' award-winning strategy was to maximize the showroom's storefront and emphasize River North's retail feel by incorporating various attention-getting elements: a striking, white spiral staircase

with mahogany treads, a reconstituted ebony veneer wall with contrasting white logo, structural columns wrapped in white acrylic, panoramic views of the Chicago River, and a product display area that exploits the window bordering the main thoroughfare, Wells Street. Happily the attractions involve more than good looks. All employees and conference rooms are located adjacent to windows and all workstations and seating are designed to ergonomic standards. With indoor air monitored for quality, and 90 percent of construction waste being diverted from landfills, Kimball Office is as wholesome—awarded LEED-CI Silver certification—as it is handsome.

Top left: Reception.

Top right: Evening view of showroom and Chicago River.

Middle left: Conference area.

Bottom left: Furniture vignette with Kimball logo.

Opposite: Entrance and spiral staircase.

Photography: Brian Gassel/ TVS Interiors.

TVS Interiors

Are quality design and environmental responsibility a good match for business? An award-winning, one-floor 7,000 square-foot Atlanta showroom leaves no doubt. The space was designed by TVS Interiors for Interface, a premium floorcoverings manufacturer and leading advocate of sustainable design. Interface's mission was to create a showroom convenient to customers, flexible for merchandising, and expressive of the company's image. It needed to be responsive to office tasks, suitable for special events, and supportive of downtown Atlanta's redevelopment. Lastly, the project had to meet demanding guidelines for LEED-CI Platinum certification. The linear space, which comprises reception, four product galleries, product presentation area,

private and open offices, touchdown area, conference room, sample room and kitchen/servery, resembles a residential loft. Its 12-foot diameter lampshades, exposed concrete floor with alternating areas of bamboo flooring, and large, billboard-size walls successfully appeal to both commercial and residential customers. These features define an environment where promotional zones are created simply by lowering shades between galleries. Ray Anderson, Interface's founder and chairman, gratefully notes, "TVS helped Interface realize a vision and achieve what was a first for us and indeed a first for our industry: a LEED-CI Platinum showroom which demonstrates for our customers in the retail and commercial design community our commitment to sustainability."

Top left: Seating area.
Top right: Street view.
Above right: Overall view.
Left: Office area and sample room.
Below left: Kitchen and touch down space.
Photography: Brian Gassel/ TVS Interiors.

VOA Associates Incorporated

224 S. Michigan Avenue
Suite 1400
Chicago, IL 60604
312.554.1400
312.554.1412 (Fax)
www.voa.com

VOA Associates Incorporated

VOA Associates Incorporated

Investment Management Company
Chicago, Illinois

"Less is more," Mies van der Rohe's Spartan credo of International Style modernism, endures even as 21st-century society struggles with oversized meals, SUVs and McMansions. An award-winning example of how a modest space can serve grand ambitions is the new, 4,000-square-foot Chicago office for seven employees of an Investment Management Company, designed by VOA Associates Incorporated. The company desired an environment that would not just accommodate all of its functions, but would feel larger as well. VOA's expertly tailored solution is defined by interlocking planes and patterns across its walls, ceilings and floors, so a simple, clean and versatile space can be folded and unfolded to alter its functions. Thus, a facility containing a reception area, private offices, conference space, administrative workstations and pantry can create new spatial configurations at will. Private offices, for example, are effortlessly transformed into spontaneous teaming areas, conference room doors pivot to serve as walls, and cabinetry and shelving open to reveal multiple layers of storage, including hidden coves. Yet the finished interiors are hardly austere, being appointed in wood, stone, and glass with graceful, minimal contemporary furnishings and subtly integrated lighting. Delighted with its new surroundings, the company insists VOA exceeded its expectations.

Top right: Built-in seating in reception.

Right: View of conference room from reception.

Opposite: Reception.

Photography: Nick Merrick/ Hedrich Blessing.

VOA Associates Incorporated

bluprint Restaurant
Chicago, Illinois

If good New American fare served by a friendly wait staff in a stylish contemporary atmosphere works its magic, the new, 200-seat, 4,450-square-foot bluprint Restaurant will give art-and-design-conscious Chicagoans a compelling reason to visit the cavernous Merchandise Mart even when they have no intention of seeing its wholesale showrooms. The arrival of bluprint, designed by VOA Associates Incorporated for Jim Horan, CEO of the Blue Plate catering company, is part of the Mart's drive to lure Windy City residents with cultural attractions. Thus, the facility, comprising a bar, dining room, bathrooms and kitchen, acts as a destination venue for the public as well as Mart tenants and their wholesale trade customers. VOA's design employs such high-gloss materials as hardwood veneers, glass and acrylic, dividing the space into smaller, more intimate areas with translucent, floor-to-ceiling panels in blue and silver, lining one area in zebra wood booths, highlighting another with white-topped communal tables, and positioning the glowing, walnut-inlaid bar at an angle that seemingly sets it in motion. A young and appreciative professional crowd has already discovered that the sculpted, angular spaces, stark, contemporary furnishings, and sophisticated indirect lighting serve as tempting eye candy even before the food arrives.

Top left: Bar.

Top right: Glass-lined area for communal tables.

Above: Booth seating area adjacent to bar.

Opposite: Perspective view of booths.

Photography: Nick Merrick/Hedrich Blessing.

VOA Associates Incorporated

Dade Behring
Customer Solutions Center
Newark, Delaware

Can a showcase for sophisticated clinical diagnostic
instruments excite visitors
as well as enlighten them?
Dade Behring, the world's
largest company dedicated
solely to clinical diagnos-
tics, and VOA Associates
Incorporated, its architect
and interior designer, have
created a new 7,000-square-
foot Customer Solutions
Center in Newark, Delaware
that can indeed. The design
of the facility, encompassing
a reception area, showroom,
representation room, conference rooms and café, allows
Dade Behring to present and
explain such products as its
flagship Vista instrument
under optimum conditions. In
addition, the award-winning
design visualizes such abstract concepts as chemistry
and science, using curvilinear
architectural shapes inspired
by the nature of a blood cell
and the flow of chemicals,
the company logo, expressed
in a glowing "DB wall" and
companion "scientific art
wall," the company's mission

Top left: Detail of "DB" wall.

Top right: Detail of center
millwork wall.

Right: Center millwork wall and
Vista instrument display.

Opposite: View of "DB" wall
and "scientific art" wall.

Photography: Nick Merrick/
Hedrich Blessing.

VOA Associates Incorporated

statement, emphasized by a "Dade Behring faces" wall that reinforces company branding materials in the presentation room, and the complex nature of science, which a center millwork wall mirrors in glowing, multi-colored cubes set at various depths. For an organization founded in the work of Dr. Emil von Behring, recipient of the first Nobel Prize for Medicine and Physiology in 1901, the facility opens a luminous doorway into its second century.

Right: Reception area.

Wirt Design Group, Inc.

617 West 7th Street
Suite 301
Los Angeles, CA 90017
213.239.0990
213.239.0991 (Fax)
info@wirtdesign.com
www.wirtdesign.com

Wirt Design Group, Inc.

Northwestern Mutual Financial Group
Los Angeles, California

What makes people feel secure? Since 1857, the subsidiaries of Northwestern Mutual Financial Group have helped clients manage financial risk and achieve financial security through insurance and investment products. To express Northwestern Mutual's concept of a "solid foundation" in a new, two-floor, 45,000-square-foot Los Angeles office, Wirt Design Group has designed its environment to project an overall sense of unity and strength while accommodating the individual consulting financial advisors who lease space from the company for themselves and their junior team and administrative and support staff. Thus, the design's contemporary "building block" motif highlights the public spaces in a facility that includes a reception area with a dramatic, interconnecting stair, perimeter private offices, open administrative areas, a conference center with conference rooms, breakout rooms and informal lounges, a training center and a lunchroom. Materials and furnishings likewise reinforce the sense of security. Such finishes as limestone, cherry wood veneer, granite, Venetian plaster, stainless steel and glass are combined with contemporary furniture, custom millwork, a neutral color scheme with vivid blue and green accents, and natural lighting that penetrates deep into interior areas to create a timeless environment that nevertheless captures the restless energy of the metropolis it serves.

Top right: Corridor.
Top left: Executive reception.
Above: Stairs and waiting area.
Lower right: Private office.
Bottom right: Open administrative area.
Opposite: Reception.
Photography: Joshua Perrin.

Wirt Design Group, Inc.

Lightfoot Vandevelde Sadowsky Crouchley Rutherford & Levine, LLP
Los Angeles, California

Small, independent and respected for its specialization in criminal defense, Lightfoot Vandevelde Sadowsky Crouchley Rutherford & Levine is a Los Angeles-based law firm that maintains its boutique status so the attorneys can practice their hands-on approach to the law. Its unique spirit is expressed in a new, 20-person, fifth-floor, 10,000-square-foot office in a renovated downtown building, designed by Wirt Design Group, that celebrates modern architecture and an impressive contemporary art collection. While the conventional floor plan places attorneys in private offices with strategically positioned break-out and conference spaces, and centralizes public functions such as reception, library and mail/copy room, the architecture is decidedly unconventional. Public functions provide an architectural context for the art collection. Ceilings are exposed to establish a gallery-like volume. Transparent and frosted glass panels allow glimpses through rooms to maintain an open atmosphere. Understated interior appointments are enriched with such accents as a bamboo hardwood floor, wenge-topped reception desk, graceful modern furniture--featuring mid-20th-century classics-

-and subtle direct/indirect lighting. Even busy attorneys take notice. As partner John D. Vandevelde, Esq., pointed out, "We are settling in and the space seems to be all we had hoped--a wonderful design, with strikingly beautiful, yet practical, space."

Above: Conference room and reception.

Right: Seating area in reception.

Opposite: Corridor and private offices.

Photography: Paul Bielenberg.

Wirt Design Group, Inc.

Yahoo!
Burbank, California

A new Burbank, California campus for Yahoo!, the popular Internet search engine, became a challenging merger of organizational cultures when the Sunnyvale-based giant began combining its Pasadena operations with those of Overture, a leading, Pasadena-based Internet search marketing firm it acquired. The planning of the Burbank campus, a two-building, five-story, 390,000-square-foot, build-to-suit development on a fast track schedule, has succeeded largely because Wirt Design Group understood the two companies' needs from the start, creating an interior design to satisfy all 1,500 employees. The design team's skills were tested when a Yahoo! executive rejected a hybrid model combining Overture's entirely open spaces and Yahoo!'s high-bay, open-plan work stations for a workplace dominated by the Yahoo! brand. Fortunately, a new concept was quickly devised featuring public zones displaying Yahoo!'s vivid and futuristic palette of purple, white and silver colors accented by such high-tech motifs as back-lit reception desks and glass panels and doors embedded with LED lights, bold colors on floors for wayfinding, and 8-foot x 8-foot open-plan work stations—with lower height panels. Thus, private offices, open-plan offices, espresso bar, training rooms, data center, quiet room, interview room and store actively support an environment where everyone does Yahoo!

Wirt Design Group, Inc.

eHarmony.com
Pasadena, California

Playing matchmaker between one of America's leading online relationship services and three office buildings vying for its corporate headquarters, Wirt Design Group recently helped 250 employees of eHarmony.com find cost-effective space in a two-floor, 45,000-square-foot facility in Pasadena. eHarmony.com's predicament commonly effects young, growing organizations. Having expanded ad-hoc over non-contiguous floors, the company gave employees little opportunity for interaction during 24/7 operations. The winning building not only offered large floorplates to place all employees on one floor, it assumed the build-out cost and provided ground-floor space at a reduced rate for company-wide meetings. However, Wirt Design Group had just four weeks to complete schematic design, design development, and construction documents for private offices, conference rooms, call center, family room, training room, audio-visual rooms, training room and lunchroom. Although company founder and clinical psychologist Dr. Neil Clark Warren favored a traditional look, the design reflects the modern tastes of the younger employees and customers in an almost completely open space of bright colors, contemporary furnishings, and colorful wall graphics featuring happy, real-life couples endorsing eHarmony.com's services. Declares John Powers, eHarmony.com's vice president of finance and administration, "Our new office is a perfect blend of functionality and style."

Above: Reception.
Top right: Conference room and reception.
Upper right: Waiting area.
Lower right: Employee entrance.
Bottom right: Call center.
Photography: Paul Bielenberg.

by Tom Newhouse

QUINdulgences

Sensuous curves.

Leather-clad bowfronts.

Delicious details.

The Quin Collection

by Tom Newhouse is

a feast for the eyes

and the soul. Crafted

in solid hardwoods, it

is infinitely renewable,

surprisingly adjustable,

justifiably indulgent.

Quin patent pending

HARDENcontract

DESIGN

QUALITY

SERVICE

A R K

Architectural Response Kollection, Inc.

www.ark-inc.com
toll free 888 241 7100
email info@ark-inc.com

Design with light.

light

www.artemide.us

systems

Artemide®
ARCHITECTURAL

Lean, Green but not Mean

By Roger Yee

To compete in the global economy, U.S. businesses and institutions are reshaping the office for a new, 21st-century way of working

Now you see it—and now you don't.

To witness the aerial maneuvers of the F-22 Raptor, the most complex fighter ever built, is to know how the world feels today when the United States projects its military power. To quote the May 2007 issue of *Air & Space*, the Raptor is "so stealthy as to be virtually undetectable, so fast (Mach 1.8) it's supersonic without lighting its afterburner, and so wired for battle that it sees the entire local theater of operations." On the other hand, Uncle Sam isn't consistently dominating the global economy. Some basic American industries, for example, are fighting for survival. The collective domestic auto sales of General Motors, Ford and Chrysler, for example, accounted for less than half of the total U.S. market for the first time ever in July 2007—dropping to 48.1 percent—as European and Asian auto makers continued to deepen their understanding of what Americans want to drive. Work in the 21st century is about being faster, cheaper and smarter, and today's office design is being profoundly reformulated to make this possible at all three stages of its preparation, from programming and planning to design development.

Fortunately, corporate America increasingly "gets it" about design as a business tool to implement winning strategies as well as create successful goods and services. "Clients now regard the office environment as an asset, and want design to support their culture as well as their work," notes Lauren Rottet, FAIA, principal of DMJM Rottet. "They are discovering that good design can make business enjoyable as well as profitable."

Above: Working hard comes with amenities like this sunken lounge at Cole & Weber United, a Seattle, WA advertising agency that seeks a good work-life balance for its young and ambitious staff.

Jofco

[Tahké. Design at Work.]

Introducing Tahké,
a beautiful, functional
and completely green
casegoods solution.
Designed for Jofco
by Jhane Barnes.

Changes in programming: How do you program what nobody can predict?

The business of business is still about making money, so the benefits of design are most readily measured through its impact on how people perform. Michael Bourque, IIDA, principal of NELSON, sees clients using office design at the programming stage as an agent of change management for such administrative initiatives as transforming workflow, re-defining business groups and encouraging teamwork. "We're seeing major, top down changes, like introducing one-size-fits-all individual work spaces, coming from chairmen who want to promote more interaction and collaboration," he reports. "It's even happening in professional services like law and accounting."

Design's potential impact goes beyond aligning office activity with corporate strategy. "Clients here in San Francisco realize that the way we work today may not apply tomorrow," says Mark Harbick, AIA, IIDA, director of design of Huntsman Architectural Group. "They want to be sure their facilities are flexible enough to accept changes in technology or business conditions. Counting heads and filing cabinets is no longer enough. If they can help designers anticipate how they want to work in the future, it could be their lifeboat."

Business concern about an unpredictable future influences programming in a number of ways. Many companies are writing shorter leases and tightening construction budgets to forestall the premature obsolescence of existing construction. "If you're an anchor tenant, you'll get inducements from your landlord to make a 10-year lease work for you," suggests Meg Osman, principal and corporate interiors practice leader of OWP/P. "Everyone else is taking out shorter leases of three, five or seven years with a two-year 'out' (escape) clause."

Simultaneously, more organizations accept the independent attitude of younger workers, who harbor few illusions about terms of employment, corporate paternalism or chances for advance-ment. The results are visible and fresh. New offices increasingly come with the right technology and space for the job, along with amenities to encourage group activity and creativity, and op-portunities to achieve a work-life balance. Work gets done when and where conditions permit, turning some facilities into 24/7 operations where people return late to finish assignments, and extending the workplace to off-site locations such as home or Starbucks.

Above: You won't find private offices at Redwood Trust, a real estate investment trust in Mill Valley, CA, because the CEO prefers dynamic, status-free open spaces over confining traditional rooms.

CONNEXIONS

designed by
FCI Design Team

Georgia State Bar designed by Lyman Davidson Dooley Inc

FURNITURE / COMMUNICATION / INNOVATION

800-708-9991   773-772-3700   FCI-OFFICE.COM

"Young people are more willing to voice their opinions than older managers," indicates Rebecca Courtney, ASID, IIDA, principal in charge of interiors of Looney Ricks Kiss. "They want the latest tools at hand and a workplace that can support their jobs." Recognizing the importance "Gen Y" workers place on good lighting, air quality, "green" design and attractive surroundings, Courtney's clients showcase their offices to spur recruitment and retention.

Changes in planning: Why should space planning matter in cyberspace?

Nobody really knows who anyone is in cyberspace, as devotees of Lonelygirl15, Fake Steve and other Internet-based celebrities eventually discover. Yet where one sits in three-dimensional space continues to matter even when virtual space defies regimentation. In the planning stage of office design, space is organized chiefly by clustering business units and individuals sharing the most interaction. "People are testing the waters and experimenting," says Courtney. "How change will affect each type of business has not settled out yet."

Is this business as usual? Managers are still reserving prime real estate along window walls for private offices. Meanwhile, general staff occupies open workstations in the interior, and staff and visitors find public areas such as reception, meeting areas, and amenities such as lounges and cafés wherever management thinks appropriate. But new variations on this formula relocate managers to private offices in the interior, so general staff enjoys direct window exposure, or place them in open workstations with everyone else. Dropping the boss into the office pool is a scheme favored by mainstream Japanese managers and progressive U.S. leaders like New York City's Mayor Michael Bloomberg that Bourque praises ("Smart people know good ideas can come from anywhere," he insists) but considers too radical for corporate America.

Look closer, however, and space planning is changing in significant ways. Boundaries are blurring, for example, as formal distinctions yield to more practical considerations. "Many companies are thinking of the workplace more like a home," Rottet explains. "The reception area can be regarded as a living room, the break room as a kitchen/dining room, and the conference room as a multi-purpose family room." When these home-like or hotel-like spaces are available, people can use them as workplace settings to focus on "head-down" tasks or assemble for impromptu gatherings or special activities.

Above: Because the reception area and main conference rooms of the Memphis, TN law office of Baker, Donelson are connected, they can create one contiguous area for business or social events.

CONNEXIONS

designed by
FCI Design Team

Wachovia designed by Jova Daniel Busby

FURNITURE / COMMUNICATION / INNOVATION

800-708-9991   773-772-3700   FCI-OFFICE.COM

Letting workers migrate through the office during the day to perform their jobs reflects management's growing conviction that giving workers access to multiple work environments supports productivity and stimulates interest. "People need flexibility," Harbick comments. "If you and your colleagues are young and cool, the CEO might want an opportunity to sit next to you where it's fun at 9:00 a.m."

Inevitably, the unrelenting shrinkage of individual spaces—open offices are now routinely sized at 6 feet by 8 feet, while enclosed offices may be set at 10 feet by 15 feet—is prompting organizations to expand the numbers and types of public areas that offer privacy and communal space. Not only are enclosed offices less numerous, smaller and typically modular, and more uniform and spare than before, but Dilbert's cubicle farm has evolved into virtually undivided space with low partitions or none at all in response to young workers' intense dislike of them. To offset this trend, Osman advises clients to stock new facilities with a range of meeting rooms, quiet rooms, touchdown stations and other enclosed spaces. "The main purpose of the office is to bring together people who drive the business," she points out. "Otherwise, people can work quite effectively outside the normal boundaries."

Changes in design: Does form really follow function in corporate design?

What's the logic of maintaining both a plush, golf course-size CEO suite for an occupant who is seldom present and a practical, telephone booth-size administrative workstation to confine its full-time occupant? It's the same logic that draws some motorists to magisterial Mercedes Benz S-Class sedans and others to sensible Honda Accords. Status--who we are in the social structure—always coexists with function—what we do for the community—in everything we design. "Status endures as a signpost in corporate offices," concludes Courtney.

Surprisingly, the expression of status is becoming muted in the design development stage of office design even as disparities in income distribution widen between senior managers and their subordinates. Bourque insists, "More CEOs want accommodations like everyone else's." Egalitarianism has its limits, nonetheless. "Top executives may not be in their offices often," Rottet concedes, "but their companies want their quarters to look appropriate to their responsibilities. True, there's less ego overall. Yet in the entertainment industry, it's all about 'me.' And young, dynamic financial firms are often very competitive about their offices."

Above: Interaction is key to online travel agency Orbitz's Chicago headquarters, so clustering private offices and teaming rooms around the core promotes corporate strategy through openness.

P A O L I ™

fuse

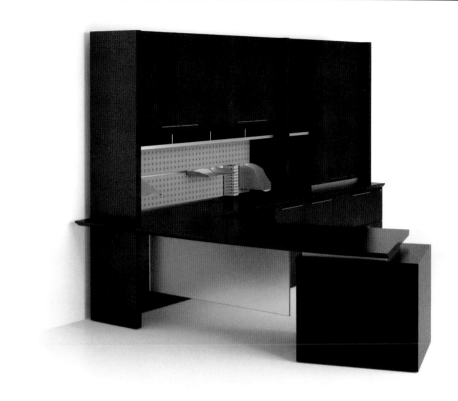

Modular with a built-in look, installs flush to wall, cabinetry choices for concealing printers and other devices.

Movable panels throughout for easy connections to wall outlets, quick wire routing, more access for installing and servicing devices.

Corporate America certainly isn't shy about branding—enlisting design to integrate visual cues about what it does ("our mission") and believes ("our values") into the workplace. The technique has its virtues. "Branding is good if done right," Harbick argues. "It reminds employees and visitors why they're at the office, and helps everyone stay on message. It's particularly useful for large, complex, multi-national operations, whose specific activities may be unknown even to many employees." Still, office workers soon tune out what Courtney calls "in your face" efforts.

Design is also respected by more businesses and institutions, architects and interior designers happily note, for creating innovative places where people want to congregate, share ideas, excel in their work, and feel pride in themselves and their organizations. The tight control of design firms through comprehensive corporate design standards, a product of the 1980s, is frequently being supplanted by corporate design guidelines open to interpretation. "Corporate design standards still make sense in certain areas where nothing is gained by reinventing the wheel, like handling the company logo," Osman admits. "But companies now realize there may be better ways to design they don't know about." Or as Rottet discloses, "Clients now give me their design standards manuals with a request to please question them."

A new partnership between business and design

Why does a business hire an architect or interior designer? Diane Hoskins, AIA, an executive director of Gensler, notes that design helped clients clarify the workflow process and address corporate image in the 1970s and 1980s. In the 1990s, design integrated technology into the workplace, confronting change, flexibility and the collapse of time and space. Now, design is striving to maximize the potential of people. "People have always been a key factor," Hoskins acknowledges. "But because of the global economy, priorities have shifted. Today, compa-

nies are facing talent wars and trying to get the most out of individual and collective effort. Design enables the client to honor the cultural context wherever its people are working, while focusing their attention on the uniqueness of their organization, products and operations worldwide."Aesthetics has its place in the new order, though it's not about making space beautiful. "Corporate design optimizes your people and your message," Hoskins continues. "What makes you stand out? Why should the customer choose you? How come your people and technologies are so effective? Those are questions design can answer visibly." In effect, Hoskins concludes, if you want your workplace to be as competitive as you are, hire a designer.

Above: Lively and thoughtful content make the branding of Baxter International's Deerfield, IL headquarters lobby via interactive displays and lounge seating enticing to both staff and visitors.

I AM ELEGANT.

←——— 2.9" ———→

I AM AMERLUX.

Discover the uncompromising performance and efficiency of Evoke 20W metal halide downlights.

I am Amerlux, the world leader in high-performance, 20W metal halide luminaires. With precision-engineered, die-cast construction and innovative optics that provide a range of tinting and beam spread options, Amerlux EcoTectural fixtures—like Evoke downlights—deliver the color and intensity of incandescent or halogen for a fraction of the energy and maintenance costs.

Available round or in a seamless square with an aperture of just 2.9", Evoke gives architects and lighting designers the flexibility to create a complete, sustainable lighting scheme—featuring general, accent, task and wall washing—using a single family of sleek, energy-efficient, specification-grade fixtures.

Evoke: I am flexible. I am dramatic. I am Amerlux.

AMERLUX®
LIGHTING SOLUTIONS

ADAPT. ABILITY.™

www.amerlux.com

Resources*

655 Broadway, San Diego, CA
Design Firm: Carrier Johnson
General Contractors: Webcor Builders
Lighting Consultants: Horton Lees Brogden
Lighting Design

**Allina Hospitals & Clinics - Corporate
Headquarters**
Design Firm: Perkins+Will
Furniture: Brayton, Herman Miller
Carpets & Flooring: Constantine, Mohawk
Fabrics: Knoll, Maharam
Lighting: Lightolier
Ceilings: Armstrong
Wallcoverings and Paint: Knoll, Sherwin-
Williams
Window Treatments: Hunter Douglas
General Contractors: Ryan Construction
Lighting Consultants: LKPB Engineers

**American Airlines Admirals Club -
JFK Int'l Airport**
Design Firm: Spillis Candela DMJM
Furniture: Brayton, Charles Alan, Ekitta
Carpets & Flooring: Collins & Aikman,
Imagine Tiles, Walker Zanger
Fabrics: Knoll, Maharam, Spinneybeck
Wallcoverings and Paint: Architectural
Systems, Blumenthal, ICI Paints, Maya Romanoff,
Southwest Progressive Enterprises
General Contractors: Cardet Construction
Co. Inc.

**AstraZeneca - Government Affairs
Department Offices**
Design Firm: Kling
Furniture: Brayton, Davis, Nienkamper,
Steelcase
Carpets & Flooring: Arc Stone, Armstrong,
Daltile, Forbo, Shaw
Lighting: Bartco, Gotham, Kurt Versen, Lithonia,
RSA Lighting, Selux
Ceilings: Armstrong
Wallcoverings and Paint: Benjamin Moore,
Daltile, Designtex, Duroplex, Maharam, Zolatone
Window Treatments: Maharam
General Contractors: Sigel Construction
Corporation
Lighting Consultants: Kling

America Online
Design Firm: Ted Moudis Associates
Furniture: Haworth
Carpets & Flooring: Interface
Fabrics: Maharam
Lighting: LED, Mark Lighting
Window Treatments: Levelor, MechoShade
General Contractors: StructureTone

Ardmore Partners
Design Firm: Meyer Design, Inc.
Furniture: Herman Miller, Source
Carpets & Flooring: Amtico, J&J Invision
Fabrics: ArcCom
Lighting: Delta
Wallcoverings and Paint: Wolf Gordon
General Contractors: R.H. Reinhardt

Attalus Capital
Design Firm: Meyer Design, Inc.
Furniture: HBF, Herman Miller, OFS
Carpets & Flooring: Armstrong, ASI Hardwood
Flooring, Durkan, Expanko, Mohawk, Robin Reig
Lighting: Cooper Lighting, Eureka, Focal Point,
Lightolier, Metalux, Radiant
Ceilings: Armstrong
Wallcoverings and Paint: Benjamin Moore,
Campherwood, Maharam, 3-Form, Tabu, Wall-
talkers, Wolf Gordon
General Contractors: Murphy Quigley

**Baker, Conelson, Bearman, Caldwell and
Berkowitz, PC**
Design Firm: Looney Ricks Kiss Architects, Inc.
Furniture: Herman Miller, Knoll, South Central
Contractors
Carpets & Flooring: J&J Invision
Fabrics: Fortuny
Lighting: Headley Menzies
General Contractors: Grinder, Taber &
Grinder, Inc.

Birtcher Development & Investments
Design Firm: H. Hendy Associates
Furniture: David Edward, Geiger, Herman Miller,
McGuire
Carpets & Flooring: Karastan
Fabrics: Jhane Barnes, Pollack
Lighting: Capri, FineLite, Omega
Wallcoverings and Paint: Carnegie, Dunn
Edwards, Innovations
General Contractors: Coastal Pacific
Construction

Blue Heron Capital
Design Firm: BBG-BBGM
Furniture: Washington Workplace
Carpets & Flooring: Armstrong, Atlas, Fortune
Contract, Gammapar
Lighting: Columbia
Ceilings: Armstrong
Wallcoverings and Paint: Benjamin Moore,
Maharam, Wolf Gordon
General Contractors: Maagnum Construction

bluprint Restaurant
Design Firm: VOA Associates Incorporated
Furniture: Allemuir, Cape Contract, Davis, Knoll
Carpets & Flooring: Berger Juelle, Lavzon,
Terrazzo
Fabrics: Spinneybeck
Lighting: Kurt Versen, Lightolier, Pinnicale
Ceilings: Ecophon, Rulon
Wallcoverings and Paint: Benjamin Moore
General Contractors: W.E. O'Neil

Buchalter Nemer Los Angeles
Design Firm: POLLACK architecture
Furniture: Geiger International, Herman Miller,
Keilhauer, Nucraft
Carpets & Flooring: Masland, Shaw
Fabrics: Edelman Leather
Lighting: Boyd Lighting, Peerless, Selux, Wila
Ceilings: Armstrong
Wallcoverings and Paint: Dunn-Edwards,
Maharam, Wolf Gordon
Window Treatments: MechoShade
General Contractors: Environmental
Contracting Corporation

Capmark Finance, Inc.
Design Firm: Meyer Design, Inc.
Furniture: Hayworth, Jofco
Carpets & Flooring: Armstrong, Collins &
Aikman, Marmoleum, Milliken
Lighting: Artemide, Eureka, Focal Point,
Lightolier, Simkar
Ceilings: Armstrong
Wallcoverings and Paint: Benjamin Moore,
Marlite, Wolf Gordon
General Contractors: Berks Ridge

Carat Fusion
Design Firm: Margulies & Associates
Furniture: Jofco, Kimball, NuCraft, Steelcase,
Wilkhan
Carpets & Flooring: Atlas, Shaw

*An Incomplete list of major sources.
For more information please call design firms.

282

CREATIVE
FURNITURE SOLUTIONS
FOR CORPORATE
ENVIRONMENTS

VS America, Inc.:
1940 Abbott Street, Unit 501
Charlotte, NC 28203
Phone: 704-378-6500
Fax: 704-378-6005

info@vs-furniture.com
www.vs-furniture.com

Fabrics: Architex, Maharam
Lighting: Color Kinetics, Focal Point, Hampstead
Ceilings: USG
Wallcoverings and Paint: Benjamin Moore, Koroseal
General Contractors: StructureTone
Lighting Consultants: Margulies & Associates

ConocoPhillips
Design Firm: Planning Design Research Corporation
Furniture: Bernhardt, Brochsteins Inc., Davis, Steelcase, Zographous
Carpets & Flooring: Bentley, Interface
Fabrics: Knoll, Maharam, Spinneybeck
Lighting: Lightolier, Lucifer, Peerless
Ceilings: Armstrong, Decoustics, Eurospan
Wallcoverings and Paint: Benjamin Moore, Knoll
Window Treatments: MechoShade
General Contractors: W.S. Bellows Construction
Lighting Consultants: Planning Design Research Corporation, Quinten Thomas Associates

Country Music Television
Design Firm: TVS Interiors
Furniture: Brayton, Brent Comber, Keilhauer, Knoll, Retromodern, Teknion, Vecta
Carpets & Flooring: Interface
Fabrics: Brayton, Carnegie, Luna, Unika Vaev
Lighting: Alkco, Barco, Bruck, Celestial, Flos, Gammalux, Lithonia, Louis Poulsen, Lucifer, Prescolite, Puck, Specialty Lighting, Zumtobel
Wallcoverings and Paint: Benjamin Moore, ICI, Walltalker, Wolf Gordon
General Contractors: Brasfield & Gorrie
Lighting Consultants: Quentin Thomas Associates, Inc.

Crevier Classic Car Company
Design Firm: H. Hendy Associates
Furniture: Baker, Barclay, Butera
Carpets & Flooring: Stark Carpets, Walker Zanger, Zaxxon
Fabrics: Barclay, Butera, Osborne & Little
Lighting: Lithonia, Winona
Ceilings: Armstrong
Wallcoverings and Paint: Innovations, Oceanside Glass Tile, Wolf Gordon
Window Treatments: Designtex, Sheward & Sons
General Contractors: JLC Associates

Cushman & Wakefield
Design Firm: DMJM Rottet
Furniture: HBF, Kimball, Knoll
Carpets & Flooring: Constantine, Solutia
Fabrics: Knoll, Maharam, Spinneybeck
Ceilings: USG
Wallcoverings and Paint: Knoll
General Contractors: Taslimi Construction
Lighting Consultants: Horton Lees Brogden

Dade Behring
Design Firm: VOA Associates Incorporated
Furniture: ICF, Keilhauer, Knoll, Nienkamper, Vecta
Carpets & Flooring: Constantine
Fabrics: Knoll, Spinneybeck
Lighting: Cooper Lighting, Eureka, Focal Point, Lucifer, Peerless, Square One, Zumtobel
Ceilings: Armstrong
Wallcoverings and Paint: Benjamin Moore
General Contractors: S.C. & A. Construction, Inc.

Edelman Financial Services
Design Firm: BBG-BBGM
Furniture: Herman Miller
Carpets & Flooring: Armstrong, Atlas, Masland
Lighting: Lightolier
Ceilings: Armstrong
Wallcoverings and Paint: Benjamin Moore, Wolf Gordon
General Contractors: Rand Construction
Lighting Consultants: CM Kling & Associates

eHarmony
Design Firm: Wirt Design Group, Inc.
Furniture: Knoll
Carpets & Flooring: J&J Invision
Fabrics: Knoll
Lighting: Lightolier
Ceilings: Armstrong
Wallcoverings and Paint: Koroseal, Sherwin Williams
General Contractors: Corporate Contractors

Executive Headquarters for a Fortune 100 Company
Design Firm: DMJM Rottet
Furniture: Bernhardt, Brayton, Decca, Martin Brattrud, Steelcase
Carpets & Flooring: American Olean, Armstrong, Daltile, Expanko, Forbo, Marble Systems, Masland, Shaw, Stone Source, Tuva Looms
Fabrics: Bergamo, Designtex, HBF, Hunt, Maharam, Pollack, Spinneybeck, Steelcase, Valley Forge
Ceilings: Armstrong, Eurospan
Wallcoverings and Paint: Hemp Traders, Holland & Sherry, Imperial Woodworking, Jim Thompson, Sccuffmaster, Sherwin Williams, Valley Craftsmen, Wallcoverings International
Staircase: A-Val Architectural Metal Corp.
Window Treatments: Bergamo
General Contractors: Basic Builders, Inc.

FedExForum Suite
Design Firm: Looney Ricks Kiss Architects, Inc.
Furniture: Bernhardt
Carpets & Flooring: Edward Fields
Fabrics: Designtex, Knoll, Shashi Caan
Lighting: Bruck, LBL Lighting, Tech Lighting
Ceilings: Armstrong
Wallcoverings and Paint: Dawn Hamm Studio
General Contractors: Mortenson

First Horizon National Corporation Hdqtrs
Design Firm: Looney Ricks Kiss Architects, Inc.
Furniture: Bernhardt, Custom Woodcrafts, David Edward, Falcon, FCS, HBF
Carpets & Flooring: Invision, Monterey
Fabrics: Daniel Duross Leather, Designtex, HBF, Spinneybeck
Lighting: LBL Lighting
Ceilings: Custom Woodcrafts, Decoustics
Wallcoverings and Paint: Sanitas, Scuffmaster, Tapetex, Whisperwalls, Wolf Gordon
Window Treatments: Maharam, S. Harris
General Contractors: Grinder, Taber & Grinder, Inc.

Four Seasons Venture Capital
Design Firm: BBG-BBGM
Carpets & Flooring: Monterey, Wicanders
Lighting: Lightolier
Ceilings: Armstrong
Wallcoverings and Paint: Benjamin Moore, Genesis, Wicanders
Window Treatments: MechoShade
General Contractors: Peris Construction

Gebhardt & Smith, LLP
Design Firm: Francis Cauffman
Furniture: Baker, HBF, Tella
Carpets & Flooring: Armstrong, Blue Ridge, Constantine, Durkan, Masland, Mohawk, Stone Source
Fabrics: HBF, Pollack, Rodolph
Lighting: Boyd Lighting, Focal Point, Gotham, Lithonia, Lucifer, RSA, Selux, Zumtobel

Ceilings: Armstrong, USG
Wallcoverings and Paint: Benjamin Moore, Carnegie, Designtex, Knoll, MAB, Maharam, Pollack, Scuffmaster
Window Treatments: HBF Textiles
General Contractors: Constantine Commercial
Lighting Consultants: The Lighting Practice

General Motors Government Relations Office
Design Firm: RTKL Associates Inc.
Furniture: Davis, Geiger International, Herman Miller, Nienkamper, Metro, VOX
Carpets & Flooring: Armstrong, Caesar, Constantine, Lonseal, Shaw, Stone Source
Fabrics: Carnegie, Dauphine, Edelman Leather, HBF, Knoll, Luna, Maharam,
Lighting: Focal Point, Lithonia, Steng Lighting, Zumtobel
Ceilings: Ecophon, USG
Wallcoverings and Paint: Benjamin Moore, Innovations, Maharam, Sherwin Williams, Walltalkers
General Contractors: Forrester Construction Company
Lighting Consultants: RTKL Associates Inc.

Greenberg Traurig LLP
Design Firm: Francis Cauffman
Furniture: Geiger International, Knoll
Carpets & Flooring: Atlas, Constantine, Forbo, J&J Commercial, Stone Source
Fabrics: Knoll, Pollack, Spinneybeck
Lighting: Delta, Focal Point, Lightolier, Lithonia, Neoray, Peerless, RSA Lighting, Selux, Spectrum, Tre Ci Luce
Ceilings: Armstrong, USG
Wallcoverings and Paint: Benjamin Moore, Knoll, Maharam, OnePlusOne, Scuffmaster, Sherwin Williams, Zolotone
Window Treatments: MechoShade
General Contractors: BPG Construction
Lighting Consultants: The Lighting Practice

Haworth Showroom
Design Firm: Perkins+Will
Furniture: Haworth
Carpets & Flooring: Bisazza Tile, Lees, Masland
Fabrics: Carnegie, Luna Textiles, Maharam
Lighting: Color Kinetics, Exterieur Vert, Lightolier, Louis Poulsen, Prudential
Ceilings: Armstrong
Wallcoverings and Paint: Benjamin Moore, Skyline Design, Xibitz

Window Treatments: Carnegie, MechoShade
General Contractors: Turner Construction Company
Lighting Consultants: Illuminart

Hershey Entertainment Center
Design Firm: Sasaki Associates Inc.
Furniture: Bernhardt, Keilhauer, Martin Bratrud, Steelcase
Carpets & Flooring: Armstrong, Brucewood Flooring, Interface, Karastan
Fabrics: Architex, Bernhardt, Designtex, Maharam, Spinneybeck
Lighting: Columbia Lighting, Focal Point, Leucos, Prescolite, Tan-Go
Ceilings: Ecophon, USG
Wallcoverings and Paint: Benjamin Moore, Daltile, ICI, Maharam, Pennsylvania Blueston
Window Treatments: Brentano
General Contractors: High Construction Company
Lighting Consultants: LAM Partners, Inc.

Impac
Design Firm: H. Hendy Associates
Furniture: HBF, Keilhauer, Kimball, Moen Woodworks, Office Furniture Group
Carpets & Flooring: Bentley, Collins & Aikman, Daltile, Johnsonite, Shaw, Zaxxon
Fabrics: ArcCom, HBF
Lighting: Boyd, Illuminating Experiences, Light Control, Lithonia, Winona
General Contractors: Swinterton Builders
Lighting Consultants: California Lighting Sales

Institute of Transportation Engineers
Design Firm: BBG-BBGM
Furniture: Steelcase
Carpets & Flooring: Interface, PermaGrain
Lighting: Lightolier
Ceilings: Ecophon
Wallcoverings and Paint: Duron
Window Treatments: Knoll
General Contractors: Caliber Construction
Lighting Consultants: CM Kling & Associates

Inter-American Development Bank
Design Firm: RTKL Associates Inc.
Furniture: Hussey
Carpets & Flooring: Constantine
Fabrics: Maharam
Lighting: Artemide, Belfer, Cooper Lighting, Energie Lighting, Lumiere, Metalux, Neoray, Portfolio, Surelites
Ceilings: Armstrong

Wallcoverings and Paint: Novawall, Sherwin Williams
General Contractors: The Whiting-Turner Company
Lighting Consultants: RTKL Associates Inc.

Interface Showroom and Offices
Design Firm: TVS Interiors
Furniture: B&B Italia, Charles McMurray, Geiger, HBF, Herman Miller, Kimball, Knoll, Nienkamper, Vecta
Carpets & Flooring: Constantine, Interface
Fabrics: Gretchen Bellinger, HBF, Luna, Pellicle, Spinneybeck
Lighting: Lutron, Tango
Wallcoverings and Paint: ICI, Momentum, Pittsburgh Paints, Stratford Hall

International Energy Company
Design Firm: Planning Design Research Corporation
Furniture: Brochsteins Inc., Cassina, HBF, Herman Miller, Knoll
Carpets & Flooring: Karastan
Fabrics: Carnegie, Knoll, Maharam, Spinneybeck
Lighting: Lucifer
Ceilings: Armstrong, Decoustics
Wallcoverings and Paint: Benjamin Moore, Knoll, Maharam
Window Treatments: Carnegie, Knoll
General Contractors: SpawMaxwell
Lighting Consultants: Planning Design Research Corporation

Investment Firm, Greenwich, CT
Design Firm: Roger Ferris + Partners, LLC
Furniture: Bernhardt, Geiger
Carpets & Flooring: Bentley/Prince Street, Bolyu, Constantine
Fabrics: Knoll
Lighting: Bartco, Kurt Versen, Zumtobel
Ceilings: Armstrong, Ecophon
Wallcoverings and Paint: Benjamin Moore
Window Treatments: MechoShade
General Contractors: A.P. Construction
Lighting Consultants: Roger Ferris + Partners, LLC

Investment Management Firm
Design Firm: VOA Associates Incorporated
Furniture: Niemkamper, Pirenti & Raffaeli, Vitro
Carpets & Flooring: FCI, Harbinger
Fabrics: Carrara Marble
Lighting: Alkco, Halo, Skyline Design
Ceilings: Acous Tile

DIMENSIONS

PATTERNS AND PROFILES COMBINED TO CREATE
UNIQUE DIMENSIONAL DESIGNS IN FLOORING

Spring 2006 marks the inception of the most innovative
flooring product in the rubber market to date –
Roppe Dimensions Rubber Tile. Over a year of extensive
research and development went into this product to ensure
that Dimensions would meet the needs of our ever changing
interior space requirements.

What began as a concept to take familiar shapes and patterns
provided by other popular flooring materials and make them
in a resilient rubber tile, has become the best innovation the
rubber flooring market has seen in decades. The three profiles
available are Random, Stripe and Crackle. All patterns are
familiar in design, but now available with the added benefits
that can be found only in rubber flooring products – inherent
slip resistance, comfort under foot, sound deadening qualities,
enhanced ROI in comparison to other flooring options and
their required maintenance procedures.

WITH ROPPE THE POSSIBILITIES ARE ENDLESS.
YOU DESIGN IT AND WE'LL HELP YOU MAKE IT HAPPEN.

ROPPE

Proven Flooring Experiences

1-800-537-9527   www.roppe.com

SINGLE
PRICE POINT

Wallcoverings and Paint: Benjamin Moore, Sherwin Williams
General Contractors: Interior Construction Group

Jansport Corporate Headquarters
Design Firm: POLLACK architecture
Furniture: Brayton, Herman Miller
Carpets & Flooring: Armstrong, Interface
Lighting: Finelite, LBL Lighting, Lightolier, Lithonia
Ceilings: Armstrong
Wallcoverings and Paint: Great Big Pictures
General Contractors: GCI Construction

Jenner & Block
Design Firm: SKB Architecture & Design
Furniture: Erik Joergensen, Fritz Hansen, Halcon, Knoll, PP Mobler
Carpets & Flooring: Bloomsburg, Karastan, Martin Patrick Evan
Fabrics: Anne Sorensen Leather, Jim Thompson, Knoll
Lighting: A-Light, Alko, Deltalight, Elliptipar, Lightolier, Louis Poulsen
Ceilings: Armstrong, USG
Wallcoverings and Paint: Benjamin Moore, USG
Window Treatments: MechoShade
General Contractors: JT Megan
Lighting Consultants: Victoria Ellis

Khronos, LLC
Design Firm: Ted Moudis Associates
Furniture: Herman Miller, Knoll, Nienkamper, Scope, Steelcase
Carpets & Flooring: Bloomsburg, Interface
Staircase: A-Val Architectural Metal Corp.
Lighting: Selux, Zumtobel
Ceilings: Ecophon
Window Treatments: DFB
General Contractors: L&K Partners

Kimball Office Showroom
Design Firm: TVS Interiors
Furniture: Kimball
Fabrics: Pollack
Lighting: Alkco, Bartco Lighting, Celestial Lighting, Eureka, Flos, Kurt Versen, Lighting Services Inc., Louis Poulsen, Lucifer, RSA, Selux, Specialty Lighting, Zumtobel
Wallcoverings and Paint: Kimball
Window Treatments: Trainor Glass Co.

General Contractors: Clune Construction
Lighting Consultants: Quentin Thomas Associates, Inc.

KKR Financial
Design Firm: Huntsman Architectural Group
Furniture: Douglas Durkin, Edelman Leather, HBF, Herman Miller, Ironies by Kate McIntyre, LaCour
Carpets & Flooring: Bentley Prince Street, Custom Tufenkian, Elements, Stone Selection, Walker Zanger
Fabrics: Ironies
Lighting: Boyd Lighting, Global Lighting, Ironies, Leucos, Peerless, RSA Lighting
Ceilings: Design Workshops
Wallcoverings and Paint: Beacon Hill, Benjamin Moore, Ironies, Nevamar, Trend USA, Wolf Gordon
Window Treatments: Fashion Draperry, Maharam
General Contractors: GCIII General Contractors
Lighting Consultants: H.F. Banks + Associates

Lightfoot Vandevelde Sadowsky Crouchley Rutherford & Levine, LLP
Design Firm: Wirt Dsign Group, Inc.
Furniture: Allsteel
Carpets & Flooring: Shaw
Fabrics: Knoll
Lighting: Lightolier
Ceilings: Armstrong
Wallcoverings and Paint: Dunn Edwards Paint
General Contractors: Warner Constructors

Lime Rock Management
Design Firm: DMJM Rottet
Furniture: Bernhardt, Decca Contract, Herman Miller
Carpets & Flooring: Karastan, Tuva, Venetino Marble
Fabrics: Cloth UK, Holland & Sherry, Maharam, Panga Panga, Randolph Hein, Sea Gate, Simba Flooring
Lighting: Spectrum
Ceilings: Armstrong, Eurospan
Wallcoverings and Paint: Pratt & Lambert
General Contractors: Basic Builders, Inc.
Lighting Consultants: DMJM Rottet

Looney Ricks Kiss Architects, Inc.
Design Firm: Looney Ricks Kiss Architects, Inc.
Furniture: Allsteel, Carolina, Haworth, Herman

Miller, Jofco, Keilhauer, Kimball, Knoll, Steelcase, Vecta
Carpets & Flooring: Interface, Jasba
Fabrics: Abet Laminati, Corian, Designtex, Donghia, Formica, Laminart, Luna Textiles, Maharam, Prismatek, Spinneybeck, 3 Form, Wilsonart
Lighting: Artemide, Corelite, Delray, Eureka, Fontana Arte, Itre, Lithonia
Ceilings: Armstrong
Wallcoverings and Paint: Armour Coat, Carnegie, Sherwin Williams,, Walltalkers
Window Treatments: Creation Bauman, Dedar, Fabricut, Maharam, MechoShade
General Contractors: Elkins Constructors

Major Insurance Company
Design Firm: Margulies & Associates
Furniture: Brayton, KI, Haworth, Metro, Steelcase, Vecta, Versteel, Wendl
Carpets & Flooring: American Olean, Crossville, Daltile, Forbo, Interface, Rikoff Quartz
Fabrics: Designtex, Haworth, KI
Lighting: Alera Lighting, Columbia, Delray, Delta, Insight, Lightolier, Louis Poulsen, Mark Lighting, Peerless, Prudential, Sistemlux, Tech Lighting, Tre Ci Luce, Wila
Ceilings: Armstrong
Wallcoverings and Paint: American Olean, Benjamin Moore, Daltile, Ecospec, Globus Cork, Maharam
Window Treatments: Draper
General Contractors: Macomber Builders
Lighting Consultants: Lisa Zeidel

Mansueto Ventures
Design Firm: TPG Architecture
Furniture: Davis, Humanscale, Kirkus, Lipse, Unifor
Carpets & Flooring: Atlas, Monterey
Fabrics: Knoll, Willow Tex Izit
Lighting: Mark Lighting
General Contractors: Lehr Construction

McNeil Consumer Healthcare
Design Firm: Francis Cauffman
Furniture: Brayton, Herman Miller, Knoll, Metro, Steelcase, Vecta
Carpets & Flooring: Forbo, Interface, Mannington, Prince Street
Fabrics: Arcchitex, Bernhardt, Designtex, Knoll, Maharam
Lighting: Artimede, Focal Point, Lightolier, Louis Poulsen
Ceilings: Armstrong
Wallcoverings and Paint: Deesigntex, Knoll,

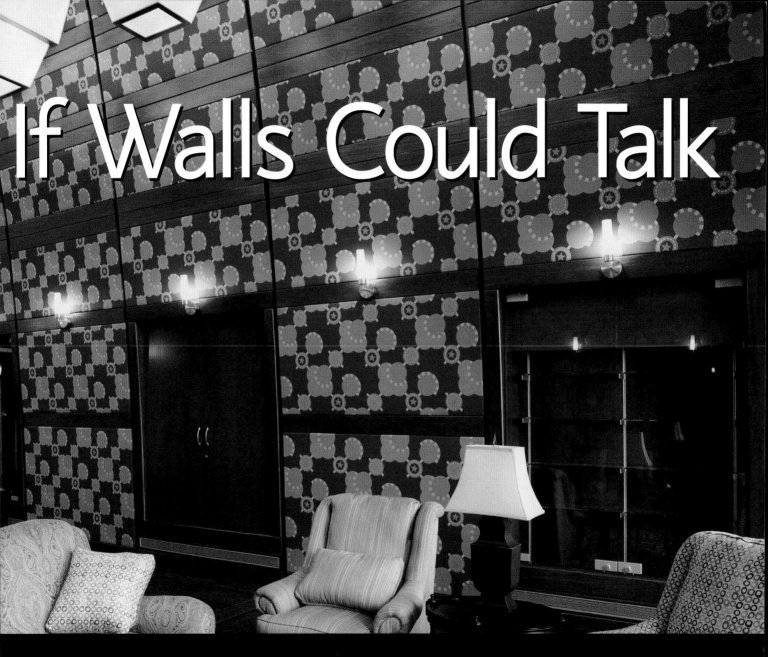

If Walls Could Talk

Walls and ceilings would request Novawall® stretch fabric coverings, the system with sustainable LEED credit attributes.

MAB Paints, Maharam, Sherwin Williams
Window Treatments: Levolor
General Contractors: Shields Construction

McNeil Nutritionals
Design Firm: Francis Cauffman
Furniture: Brayton, Herman Miller, Metro, Steelcase, Turnstone
Carpets & Flooring: Atlas, Prince Street
Fabrics: Architex, Designtex, Knoll, Maharam, Sina Pearson
Lighting: Artimede, Focal Point, Lightolier, Neoteck Lighting, Novitas
Ceilings: Armstrong
Wallcoverings and Paint: Designtex, Knoll, MAB, Maharam
General Contractors: W.M. Drayton Company

The Mechanics Bank
Design Firm: POLLACK architecture
Furniture: Bernhardt, Clervi Marble, DFlm, Lloyd Gordon Mfg., National
Carpets & Flooring: DalTile, Invision, Rossi USA Corp.
Fabrics: Bernhardt
Lighting: Alkco, Artemide, Erco, Linear Lighting, Lithonia, Louis Poulsen, Metalux, Neoray
Ceilings: USG, Ventwood
Wallcoverings and Paint: Area Code Plaster, Bizazza Tile, ICI
Window Treatments: Maharam, Silent Gliss
General Contractors: Marvin Collins Corporation
Lighting Consultants: Flack + Kurtz

Miller & Chevalier
Design Firm: SKB Architecture & Design
Furniture: Charles McMurray, Cumberland, D'Apostrophe, Geiger, Halcon, Herman Miller, ICF, Keilhauer, Knoll, Kreiss Collection, Mattaliano, Meridian, Minotti, Patella, Poltrona Frau, Prismatique, Vesta, Vitra, Wilkhahn
Carpets & Flooring: Armstrong, Boylu, Forbo, Tuva
Fabrics: ArcCom, Edelman Leather, HBF Textiles, Joseph Noble, Larsen, Poltrona Frau Leather, Unika Vaev
Lighting: Delltalight, Edison Price, Lightolier, Zumtobel
Ceilings: Armstrong, USG
Wallcoverings and Paint: Benjamin Moore, Jim Thompson, Knoll, Maharam, Wolf Gordon
Window Treatments: MechoShade

General Contractors: Rand Construction
Lighting Consultants: Victoria Ellis Consulting

Monitor Group
Design Firm: Sasaki Associates Inc.
Furniture: Allermuir, Bernhardt, Davis, HBF, Herman Miller, VS America, Watson
Carpets & Flooring: Bentley Prince Street, Johnsonite, Shaw
Fabrics: Knoll, Lucia Cassa, Luna, Pollack
Lighting: Artmide, Boyd, Bruck, Finelite, Lithonia, Omega, Williams
Ceilings: Armstrong, USG
Wallcoverings and Paint: Knoll, Sherwin Williams
General Contractors: BCCI Construction Company

Moody's / KMV
Design Firm: Huntsman Architectural Group
Furniture: Bernhardt, Geiger International, Herman Miller, Tuohy
Carpets & Flooring: Constantine, GlasBac Tile, Interface, Junkers Hardwood, Merida
Fabrics: Bernhardt, Carnegie, Knoll
Lighting: Erco
Ceilings: Armstrong, Hunter Douglas
Wallcoverings and Paint: Benjamin Moore, CCarnegie, ICI, Koroseal, Scuffmaster, Xorel
Window Treatments: Knoll, MechoShade
General Contractors: BCCI Construction Company

Motorola mobilezone.chicago
Design Firm: Tanager Design Group
Furniture: Haworth
Carpets & Flooring: Collins & Aikman, Mannington
Lighting: Elliptipar, Focal Point
Ceilings: Armstrong
Wallcoverings and Paint: Carnegie, Maharam
General Contractors: Pepper Construction

Motorola SH 1
Design Firm: Tanager Design Group
Furniture: Haworth
Carpets & Flooring: Collins & Aikman, Mannington
Lighting: Bega, Focal Point, Lightology, Metalux, Portfolio
Ceilings: Armstrong
Wallcoverings and Paint: Carnegie, Maharam
General Contractors: Pepper Construction

National Development
Design Firm: Margulies & Associates
Furniture: Aaron, Allseating, Hudson, Knoll, NuCraft
Carpets & Flooring: Atlas, Rose Quartz Granite Tiles
Fabrics: ArcCom
Lighting: Delray, Lecos, Lightolier, Mark Lighting, Selux, Tre Ci Luce
Ceilings: Armstrong
Wallcoverings and Paint: Benjamin Moore, Maharam
Window Treatments: MechoShade
General Contractors: Cranshaw Construstion
Lighting Consultants: Lisa Zeidel

Northwestern Mutual Financial Network
Design Firm: Wirt Design Group, Inc.
Furniture: HBF, Nienkamper
Carpets & Flooring: Constantine
Fabrics: Designtex, HBF
Lighting: Lightolier
Ceilings: Armstrong
Wallcoverings and Paint: Dunn Edwards, MDC
General Contractors: Corporate Contractors

OfficeMax Headquarters
Design Firm: OWP/P
Furniture: Teknion
Carpets & Flooring: Milliken
Lighting: Energie, Lite Control, Zumtobel
Ceilings: Armstrong
Wallcoverings and Paint: Sherwin Williams, Skyline Glazing, Versa
General Contractors: Clune Construction
Lighting Consultants: OWP/P

Olympus America Inc. Headquarters
Design Firm: EwingCole
Furniture: Haworth
Carpets & Flooring: Constantine, Interface, PermaGrain, Stone Source
Fabrics: Xorel
Lighting: Lutron Lighting Control, RSA Selux
Ceilings: Armstrong, Celotex
Wallcoverings and Paint: Benjamin Moore, MAB
General Contractors: Butz
Lighting Consultants: EwingCole

One Beacon Insurance
Design Firm: Margulies & Associates
Furniture: Haworth
Carpets & Flooring: Shaw

have it both ways ...

task and ambient lighting
from a single source ...
as low as 0.6 w/sf.

no lights on the ceiling
no troffers
no pendants

www.tambient.com

© **Tambient** 2007
a division of Sylvan R. Shemitz Designs, Inc., makers of **elliptipar**

Tambient®
lighting at work™

Fabrics: Carnegie, Haworth, Maharam
Lighting: Corelight, Elliptipar, Finelight, Prescolite, Tech Lighting
Ceilings: Armstrong
Wallcoverings and Paint: Wolf Gordon
General Contractors: Erland
Lighting Consultants: Lisa Zeidel

Orbitz Headquarters
Design Firm: OWP/P
Furniture: Brayton, Haworth, Herman Miller, Knoll, Parenti & Rafaelli, Vecta
Carpets & Flooring: Quarella
Lighting: Focal Point, Lighting Vendor
Ceilings: Armstrong
Wallcoverings and Paint: Benjamin MMoore, EcoSpec, Wolf-Gordon
General Contractors: ConopCo Realty and Development
Lighting Consultants: OWP/P

Paul, Hastings, Janofsky & Walker, LLP
Design Firm: DMJM Rottet
Furniture: Allsteel, Bernhardt, Cumberland, Herman Miller, ICF, Knoll, Moroso, Nienkamper, Vitra, Wilkhahn
Carpets & Flooring: Atlas, Bentley, Constantine, Fortune, Noir St. Laurent
Fabrics: Bernhardt, Carnegie, Joseph Noble, Larsen, Maharam, Sina Pearson
Lighting: Delray, Focal Point, Gotham Lighting, Kurt Versen, Lithonia, Prudential, Sonoma, Translite
Ceilings: Armstrong, Eurospan
Wallcoverings and Paint: Benjamin Moore, Sherwin Williams
Window Treatments: Carnegie, Pollack
General Contractors: Sigal Construction Corporation
Lighting Consultants: Horton Lees Brogden Lighting Design Inc.

PG&E Corporation
Design Firm: SKB Architecture & Design
Furniture: Knoll, Teknion
Carpets & Flooring: Constantine, Ecostrong, Forbo, Shaw, Tuva
Fabrics: ArcCom, Maharam, Sina Pearson
Lighting: Alco, Beta-Calco, Erco, Lithonia, Louis Poulsen, Peerless, Prudential, Zumtobel
Ceilings: Armstrong, Decoustics
Wallcoverings and Paint: Benjamin Moore, Innovations, Luna Textiles, Sonocrete, Zolatone
Window Treatments: MechoShade

General Contractors: Girard Engineering
Lighting Consultants: Jeannine Komonosky

Pixar Animation Studio
Design Firm: Huntsman Architectural Group
Furniture: Bernhardt, Design Within Reach, Herman Miller, Knoll
Carpets & Flooring: Ardex, Bentley Prince Street, GlasBac RE Tile, High Performance, Interface, Sheet Goods, Solutia
Lighting: Bega, Delray, Delta Lighting, Focal Point, Lithonia, Louis Poulsen
Ceilings: Armstrong, Hunter Douglas, USG
Wallcoverings and Paint: Benjamin Moore, USG
Window Treatments: Kawner, 3M Window Film
General Contractors: Dome Construction

POLLACK architecture
Design Firm: POLLACK architecture
Furniture: Geiger International, Herman Miller, Knoll
Carpets & Flooring: Constantine, Interface
Fabrics: Luna Textiles, Maharam
Lighting: Erco, Peerless, Prudential
Ceilings: Armstrong
Wallcoverings and Paint: Benjamin Moore
Window Treatments: MechoShade
General Contractors: Turner Interiors
Lighting Consultants: Flack + Kurtz

Redwood Trust
Design Firm: Huntsman Architectural Group
Furniture: HBF, Herman Miller, Human Scale, Kartel, Knoll, Minotti, Plexie-craft, Sandler, Trinity Engineering
Carpets & Flooring: Ardex, Elson & Co., Rex Ray, Savik
Fabrics: Luna Textiles, Maharam
Lighting: Contech, Flos, Foscarini, Lithonia, **Louis Poulsen**
Ceilings: Wall Technology
Wallcoverings and Paint: Benjamin Moore, ICI
Window Treatments: MechoShade
General Contractors: Richlen Construction

Roger Ferris + Partners, LLC offices
Design Firm: Roger Ferris + Partners, LLC
Furniture: Knoll, Nienkamper
Carpets & Flooring: Interface
Lighting: Erco, Zumtobel
Wallcoverings and Paint: Donald Kaufman Paint

Window Treatments: MechoShade
General Contractors: Pappajohn Construction

SCA Americas North American Headquarters
Design Firm: EwingCole
Furniture: HBF, Knoll, Martttin Brattrud, Tuohy
Carpets & Flooring: Constantine, Expanko, Nora, PermaGrain
Fabrics: HBF, Knoll, Sina Pearson
Lighting: Focal Point, Kurt Versen, Lithonia, Metalumen, Pathway, WAC
Ceilings: Armstrong
Wallcoverings and Paint: Benjamin Moore, Clestra Hauserman Wall System, Interlam
Window Treatments: MechoShade
General Contractors: Turner Special Projects
Lighting Consultants: EwingCole

Schlumber Limited Headquarters
Design Firm: Planning Design Research Corporation
Furniture: Fritz Hansen, Herman Miller
Carpets & Flooring: Amtico, Armstrong, Daltile, Masland, Terrazzo, Tuva Looms
Fabrics: Knoll
Lighting: Alkco, Bartco, Elliptipar, Focal Point, LightLab, Louis Poulsen, Lucifer, Winona, Zumtobel
Ceilings: Armstrong, Decoustics, Gypsum Wallboard
Wallcoverings and Paint: Benjamin Moore, Brochsteins, Knoll, Nippon Electric Glass, Novawall, Vision Products
Window Treatments: Carnegie, Nysan
General Contractors: D.E. Harvey Builders
Lighting Consultants: Planning Design Research Corporation

Societe Generale
Design Firm: Ted Moudis Associates
Furniture: HBF, Nienkamper, Steelcase, Vecta
Carpets & Flooring: Milliken
Lighting: Lightolier, Mark Lighting
Ceilings: Armstrong
General Contractors: StructureTone

Sullivan & Worcester
Design Firm: Sasaki Associates Inc.
Furniture: Knoll, OFS
Carpets & Flooring: Atlas, Constantinee, St. Vincent Limestone
Fabrics: Knoll, Maharam
Lighting: Edison Price, Intense Lighting, Lucifer, Peerless, Sistemalux

GIANNI

CASEWORK; **2600**

SEATING: **DECORO**

COMFORTABLE IN ANY ENVIRONMENT

From the Boardroom to the General Office
Functional, Elegant, Timeless
Office Furniture in Wood

www.gianniinc.com

4615 W. Roosevelt Rd., Cicero, Il. 60804   Tel.708.863.6696   Fax.708.863.4071
Showroom 10.124 Merchandise Mart - Chicago

Ceilings: Ecophone
Wallcoverings and Paint: Benjamin Moore, Innovations, Nass Fresco Finishes
Window Treatments: Carnegie
General Contractors: StructureTone
Lighting Consultants: Schweppe Lighting, Inc.

Ted Moudis Associates
Design Firm: Ted Moudis Associates
Furniture: Bernhardt, Keilhauer, Knoll, Steelcase
Carpets & Flooring: Bentley/Prince Street, Karastan, Tai Ping
Fabrics: Luna Textiles, Textile Mania
Lighting: Lightolier, LiteLab, Mark Lighting
Ceilings: Armstrong
Wallcoverings and Paint: Benjamin Moore, Wolf Gordon
Window Treatments: Luton System, SolRShade
General Contractors: JGN Construction Corporation
Lighting Consultants: Lighting Design Collaborative

Towers Perrin
Design Firm: NELSON
Furniture: Bernhardt, Brayton, Custom Precision Millwork Inc., Haworth, Keilhauer, Krug, Nienkamper, Tuohy
Carpets & Flooring: Armstrong, Azrock, Interface, Johnsonite
Fabrics: C.F. Stinson, Formica, Knoll, Momentum, Pionite, Spinneybeck, Textus
Lighting: Cooper, Lightolier, MP Lighting
Ceilings: Armstrong, USG
Wallcoverings and Paint: Benjamin Moore, Carnegie, Designtex, Knoll, Korogaard
Window Treatments: 3M Etch Window Films

Transwestern Commercial Services Regional Office
Design Firm: OWP/P

Furniture: Decca, Haworth, Nienkamper
Carpets & Flooring: Armstrong, Marbella, Shaw
Fabrics: Haworth, Paul Brayton
Lighting: Focal Point, Gammalux, Louis Paulsen, Zumtobel
Ceilings: Armstrong, Hunter Douglas
Wallcoverings and Paint: Forbo, ICF, Walltalkers
General Contractors: ICG
Lighting Consultants: OWP/P

US Green Building Council Headquarters
Design Firm: Perkins+Will
Furniture: Haworth, Metro, Steelcase
Carpets & Flooring: Interface
Fabrics: Knoll, Maharam
Lighting: Coper, IO Lighting, Legion, LSI, Luce Plan, Mark Lighting, Metalux, Neoray, Prudential, Shaper
Ceilings: Armstrong
Wallcoverings and Paint: Benjamin Moore, Scuffmaster
General Contractors: Davis Construction
Lighting Consultants: Bliss Fasman Lighting

Waterworks Inc.
Design Firm: Roger Ferris + Partners, LLC
Furniture: Vitra
Carpets & Flooring: Interface
Fabrics: Maharam, Vitra
Lighting: Alkco, Fabulux
Wallcoverings and Paint: Benjamin Moore
Window Treatments: MechoShade
General Contractors: Trans Corporation

Whiteford, Taylor and Preston, LLP
Design Firm: RTKL Associates Inc.
Carpets & Flooring: Durkan, Shaw
Fabrics: HBF Textiles, Maharam
Ceilings: USG

Wallcoverings and Paint: Maharam, Wolf Gordon
General Contractors: Constantine Commercial Construction Inc.
Lighting Consultants: RTKL Assoociates Inc.

World Bank Country Office in Bangladesh
Design Firm: SKB Architecture & Design
Furniture: David Edward, Teknion
Carpets & Flooring: Mannington
Fabrics: ArcCom, Teknion
Lighting: Erco, Lightolier
Ceilings: Armstrong
Wallcoverings and Paint: Berger Paints
General Contractors: Joint Venture Engineers Pvt Ltd.

WXPN 88.5
Design Firm: Meyer Design, Inc.
Furniture: Herman Miller
Carpets & Flooring: Bolyu, Interface
Lighting: Guth Lighting
Wallcoverings and Paint: MDC
General Contractors: Intech

Yahoo!
Design Firm: Wirt Design Group, Inc.
Furniture: Teknion
Carpets & Flooring: Shaw
Fabrics: ICF, Knoll
Lighting: Day-Brite, Prudential
Ceilings: Armstrong, Hunter Douglas
Wallcoverings and Paint: ICI
General Contractors: Krismar Construction Co., Inc.

From Conception
to Reality

Design: DMJM Rottet • Photo: Benny Chan/Fotoworks

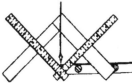

A-VAL ARCHITECTURAL METAL CORP.

Custom Ornamental Metal & Glazing Contractor

15-06 129th Street • College Point, New York, 11356

phone: 718-539-2391 • fax: 718-353-1316 • www.a-val.com

Specified Lighting Design

- New "How I Lit" Series
- LEDs in Prime Time

SPECIFIED LIGHTING DESIGN

The lighting resource for architects and designers

Providing comprehensive design and product information for lighting designers, architects, and contract interior-design professionals who specify and purchase commercial and institutional lighting.

Index by Project

The Designer Series

Visual Reference Publications, Inc.
302 Fifth Avenue, New York, NY 10001
212.279.7000 • Fax 212.279.7014 • www.visualreference.com

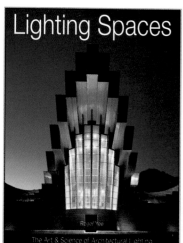

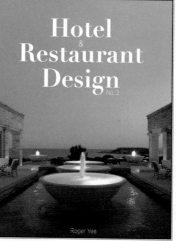

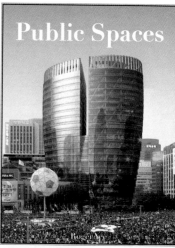

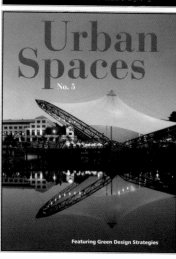

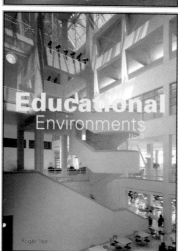

Advertiser Index